Snakes

Peter Stafford

PUBLISHED BY
THE NATURAL HISTORY MUSEUM, LONDON

First published by The Natural History Museum,
Cromwell Road, London SW7 5BD
© The Natural History Museum, London, 2000
ISBN 0-565-09149-2

A catalogue record for this book is available from
the British Library

Edited by Jonathan Elphick
Designed by Joe Hedges
Reproduction and printing by Craft Print, Singapore

DISTRIBUTION

North America, South America,
Central America and the Caribbean
Smithsonian Institution Press
470 L'Enfant Plaza
Washington D.C. 20560-0950
USA

Australia and New Zealand
CSIRO Publishing
PO Box 1139
Collingwood, Victoria 3066
Australia

UK and rest of the world
Plymbridge Distributors Ltd.
Plymbridge House, Estover Road
Plymouth, Devon PL6 7PY
UK

Contents

Preface

Few animals evoke such strong emotions in humans as snakes – they are loathed, feared, admired, or even worshipped the world over. There can be hardly anyone without at least some perception of these distinctive and fascinating animals. But what exactly is it that inspires these feelings? For many it is undoubtedly due to the fact that some snakes have deadly bites, but for most of us it is probably because they are just so difficult to comprehend. How can, after all, an animal so long and thin move so gracefully without limbs, or swallow a meal several times larger than its head, and what is it that enables some snakes to survive without eating for months or even years?

The first objective of this book is to answer some of these questions. Its other main purpose is to explore each of the main groups of snakes and convey some impression of the remarkable extent to which these animals have diversified. Snakes inhabit almost every part of the globe where temperatures remain conducive to life for at least part of the year, including the open sea, and they have become specialized for living in a wide range of different environments. Some are adapted for life in water and never venture onto dry land, while others are found only in the highest tree-tops of rainforests, or spend much of their lives burrowing underground in dry, sandy deserts. Only in the coldest regions and on some islands (notably Ireland and New Zealand) are there none at all. Equally varied and complex are the ways in which individual species live, and by focussing on aspects of their ecology I hope that the book will encourage the growing appreciation of snakes as an important group of animals that should be valued and admired rather than feared and hated.

The author

Peter Stafford has held a keen interest in amphibians and reptiles, particularly snakes, since a boy, and has been involved with studies on the biology of these animals for many years. Among his numerous publications he is credited with having written or co-authored several books on the subject of herpetology, including *The Adder*, a popular book on the natural history of this venomous snake in Britain, and most recently a comprehensive guide to the reptiles found in Belize, Central America.

Over the past ten years he has undertaken regular expeditions to Belize, and it is here where his research interests continue to be mainly focussed; his experiences studying the diverse range of snakes found there also lie partly behind the inspiration for this book. Peter is a member of several herpetological societies and the editor of the *British Herpetological Society Bulletin*. He is a pollen biologist in the Department of Botany at The Natural History Museum, London.

Structure and Lifestyle

There are about 2930 species of snakes alive today. They range from small creatures like the burrowing blind snakes that may be as little as 10 cm (4 in) long to giants such as the larger pythons and boas that grow to 7 m (23 ft) or more. Some specialized tree-living kinds are ridiculously long and thin, whereas many of the vipers, boas, and pythons are relatively short and heavy-set, and there is a whole range of different combinations in between.

While they all vary in size, shape and form, the features that collectively distinguish snakes as a group are however, clearly recognizable: the body is greatly lengthened and highly flexible, there are no apparent limbs, and the eyes have no eyelids. They differ further in lacking any sign of a shoulder girdle, forelimbs, and a sternum (breastbone), and in the vast majority there are no vestiges either of a pelvis or hind limbs; only in pythons, boas, and some other primitive forms are there remains of hind limbs, which appear externally as small, horn-like claws at the base of the tail, and some traces of a pelvis.

The earliest snakes

Biologists generally agree that snakes arose from lizard-like ancestors. Their long body shape and lack of limbs probably evolved because it enabled them to move more effectively underground or in dense vegetation, and several families of lizards include species living today that also exhibit these features. Snakes first appeared on earth during the Lower Cretaceous period, 100–150 million years ago.

The earliest remains identified as having definitely belonged to a snake originate from the Lower Cretaceous deposits of North Africa, although the species that was described on the basis of these, *Lapparentophis defrennei*, shows no link with earlier snake-like reptiles, and its precise origins have yet to be established. Only its vertebrae have survived, but the complete skeleton of a later species, *Dinilysia patagonica*, unearthed from the Upper Cretaceous sandstone beds of Argentina, sheds more light on the possible origins of

BELOW: **The ancestors of snakes may have looked very much like the slow-worm, *Anguis fragilis*, a lizard that, like snakes, has lost its legs and acquired an elongate body.**

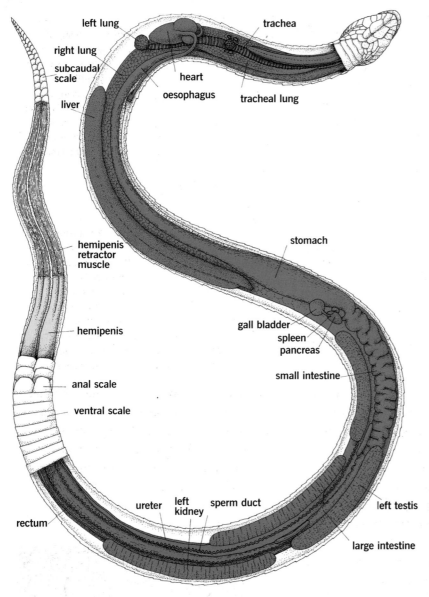

left lung

right lung

subcaudal
scale

liver

trachea

heart

oesophagus

tracheal lung

hemipenis
retractor
muscle

stomach

hemipenis

gall bladder

spleen

pancreas

small intestine

anal scale

ventral scale

rectum

ureter

left
kidney

sperm duct

left testis

large intestine

The anatomy of a snake.

snakes. *Dinilysia* is about 1.8 m (6 ft) long and, whereas in some features it resembles a lizard, it also bears similarities to the modern-day pipe snakes (families Aniliidae, Cylindrophiidae, and Anomochilidae). Some early snakes may well have looked like pipe snakes and lived as these species do now, mostly underground. Recent research, however, implies instead that these and other burrowing snakes acquired their characteristic features after the evolution of a large surface-active or perhaps aquatic ancestor.

Anatomy

Internal modifications

Over the course of evolution, elongation of the snake's body has necessitated the modification and rearrangement of its internal organs. Most of the main organs themselves are all there and not very different from those of humans; it is just that they have changed so much in shape it can be difficult to recognize them.

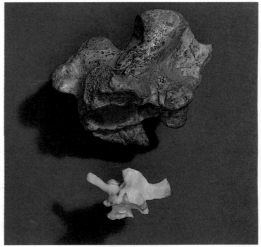

RIGHT: Snakes of the past were perhaps even larger than those in existence today. Compare this fossilized neck vertebrae of an extinct giant palaeophid snake (top) with that of a 6.6 m (21.6 ft) long reticulated python (below).

LEFT: **A snake's skeleton is comprised mostly of vertebrae and pairs of ribs. There is no sternum, shoulder girdle, or forelimbs, although in some, such as this Asian rock python,** *Python molurus*, **vestiges of the pelvis and hind limbs remain.**

BELOW: **Hemipenes of a coral snake. Biologists often use these structures to help distinguish different species of snakes, as they show great variation between species but are usually very constant within an individual species.**

The lungs in particular have undergone considerable modification. A few snakes have two lungs, but in the majority the left lung has been either lost or become greatly reduced to the extent that it no longer serves any useful purpose. Snakes breathe using the right lung alone, and in some aquatic groups, such as the file snakes, this is particularly large, extending backwards for nearly the entire length of the body. Additional respiratory area is provided by a special tube-like extension of the windpipe, known as the tracheal lung.

Among other organs affected by the radical change in body shape is the stomach, which has become greatly enlarged and in some snakes accounts for more than one-third of the total length. There is also no urinary bladder; nitrogenous waste is voided not in a solution of urea, as in humans and almost all other mammals, but in a semi-solid state as uric acid, as in lizards and birds. The heart has three chambers, as opposed to four in humans, while the male reproductive organ is an elaborate pair of structures, called hemipenes, variously adorned with frills and hooks.

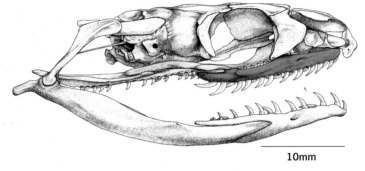

a.

10mm

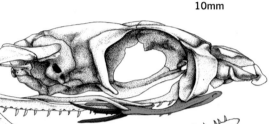

b.

10mm

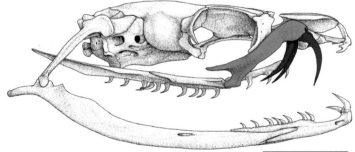

c.

10mm

Skull and teeth

The most distinctive feature of the skull in snakes is its remarkably flexible construction. With some exceptions (e.g. pipe snakes), a snake's skull bones are movably connected to each other and attached only loosely to the braincase, so that virtually the whole head is capable of being stretched and distorted in

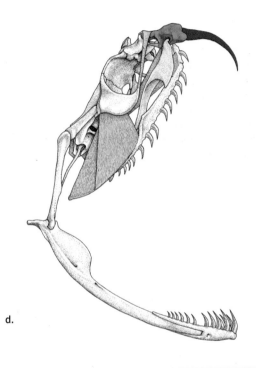

d.

■	venom-injecting fang(s)
▦	maxilla
☐	ectopterygoid
▨	principal fang erection and retraction muscles/ligaments

Types of dentition in snakes. Features shaded represent the main components of the biting mechanism; note in particular the relative sizes of the maxillary bone. (a) Non-venomous with no enlarged fangs (aglyphous). Includes blind snakes and all other primitive burrowing species, sunbeam snakes, boas, pythons, and many colubrids. (b) Venomous with enlarged, rear-mounted fangs usually preceded on the maxilla by several smaller, unmodified teeth (opisthoglyphous). Includes most burrowing asps (Aparallactinae) and many colubrids. (c) Venomous with enlarged, forward-mounted fangs that are non-erectile (proteroglyphous). Includes cobras, mambas, coral snakes, and all other elapids. (d) Venomous with enlarged, forward-mounted fangs that are erectile and capable of being pivoted independently (solenoglyphous); when not in use the fangs fold back along the upper jaw. Includes stiletto snakes (*Atractaspis*) and all vipers.

almost any direction. The two halves of the lower jaw are not fused at the front into a solid 'chin', but separated by elastic ligaments that allow them to be pushed apart when the snake is swallowing. The suppleness of the lower jaw is further enhanced by a joint in the middle of each of its two halves that enables them to be flexed outwards. Where they articulate on the side of the skull, further modifications make it possible for the two halves of the lower jaws to temporarily 'separate' and be pushed apart to allow prey to pass into the throat.

The teeth of snakes are thorn-shaped and some species may have a great many of them. As well as those lining each of the upper and lower jaws, there are normally two further rows on the inner bones of the palate (the palatine and pterygoid bones). Burrowing asps, some colubrids, elapid snakes and the vipers have one or more enlarged teeth that are specially modified for injecting venom (see p. 8, 59), and the teeth of certain other species are suited for eating particular kinds of prey. Those of the Central American neck-banded snake (*Scaphiodontophis annulatus*), for example, are slightly flattened at their tips for grasping the smooth, hard-scaled bodies of skinks on which it largely feeds. The teeth of this snake are also hinged on flexible ligaments that enable them to be locked into a backward-pointing position when prey is being swallowed, thus preventing it from struggling free.

BELOW: **Skull of a python,** *Python sebae*. **Annotations refer to bones specifically mentioned in this book. Note in particular the coronoid bone, a feature of the lower jaw retained by primitive snakes but lost in the more advanced species.**

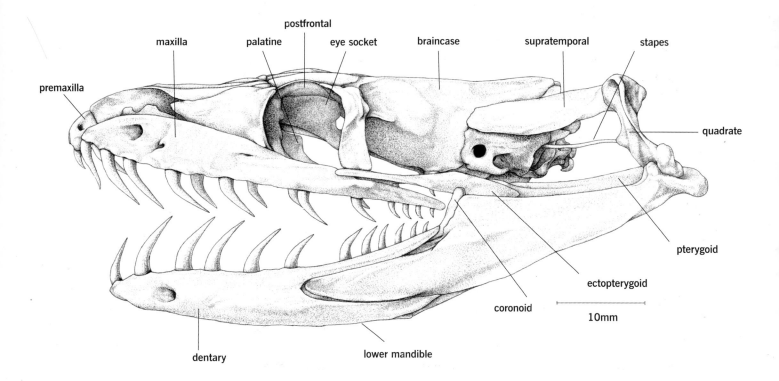

premaxilla · maxilla · postfrontal · palatine · eye socket · braincase · supratemporal · stapes · quadrate · pterygoid · ectopterygoid · coronoid · 10mm · dentary · lower mandible

Skin, scales, and moulting

As in all reptiles, the entire surface of a snake's body is covered with scales. On the head these may be large and arranged in a symmetrical pattern, or small and irregular. Those on the upper surface of the body (dorsals) are usually small and triangular, often with a horizontal ridge through the centre (keeled), while the scales on the abdomen (ventrals) are typically large and extend crosswise in a single row between the head and base of the tail. In some snakes the scales beneath the tail (subcaudals) are also arranged in a single row, while in others they form pairs. In some snakes the scales of the snout and chin are covered with microscopic sensory tubercles that appear to be associated with reproduction, and similar tubercles occur near the base of the tail in certain New World coral snakes.

The outermost layer of a snake's skin consists of a continuous sheet of keratin, a rather inflexible material also found in your fingernails and hair. Derived from dead cells, this layer must be shed every so often to allow for growth. The frequency with which this shedding, or sloughing, occurs, depends primarily on the rate of growth, and young healthy snakes, which grow more quickly, slough their skins more often.

In the initial stages of this process, the skin loses its usual fresh appearance and turns milky-white, due to the secretion of a lubricant beneath the redundant upper layer:

RIGHT: **Each individual scale of a snake's body is separated by interconnecting folds of skin concealed beneath; it is partly this which allows for the considerable flexibility needed when, e.g. the snake is consuming a large meal.**

Highly-prized skins

Snake skin is admired the world over for its attractive colours and patterns, and has been highly prized by the leather industry ever since large-scale commercial harvesting of these animals began in the early 1900s. Many species are exploited for this purpose, but none more heavily than the reticulated python (*Python reticulatus*), of which thousands are exported each year. During a six-year period between 1980 and 1985, the total estimated number of reticulated pythons exported from their native habitats was an incredible 2,299,037, which averages out at 383,173 per year. Of this number, 52,364 were live snakes, presumably destined for the pet trade, exhibition in zoos, and laboratory use, while the remainder were exported either as raw skins or processed products (mainly shoes, boots, and handbags). In recent years the number of these pythons taken from the wild has started to decline, although whether this is the result of reduced exploitation, or because populations have become so severely depleted that there are simply not so many snakes around, is unknown.

The sheer volume of snakes known to have been harvested for their skins during certain years is alarming. Based on the number reported to the Convention on International Trade in Endangered Species of Wild Flora and Fauna (CITES), the body that regulates trade in wildlife, conservationists have calculated that in 1985, for example, the leather industry used 1,449,475 m of snake skin – that is, almost 1450 km (885 miles)! Furthermore, this is an extremely conservative estimate as it includes only anacondas and large pythons, and not the many other, smaller snake species exploited for this purpose, such as boa constrictors, various Asian rat snakes, short-tailed pythons, file snakes, cobras and sea snakes. Consequently, this figure could easily represent just a small fraction of the actual number. Clifford Pope, a famous herpetologist, even once speculated that if the number of skins harvested each year were joined together to make one continuous leather belt, it would stretch around the entire world!

this is especially pronounced over the eyes. It persists for several days and may take up to three weeks before it finally clears, during which time the snake is often unable to see properly and will usually remain hidden away. Many snakes also refuse to feed during this period, and if disturbed may be aggressive.

A few days after fully regaining its sight, the snake becomes restless and begins to rub its head against the ground, stones, or other rough surfaces until the old skin separates at the tip of the snout and along the jawline, from where it then peels back over the rest of the body as the snake moves around. In the process, the old skin turns itself completely inside out. Aquatic snakes that live in open water, such as sea snakes, cannot always find suitable rough surfaces, but some of these species have ingeniously side-stepped the problem by coiling into knots and rubbing one part of the body against another.

BELOW: **Snakes identify smells using the tongue and a special organ in the roof of the mouth, Jacobson's organ. The tongue may also have a tactile function**

Senses of snakes

Smell and Jacobson's organ

Snakes have an acute sense of chemoreception (odour detection), although they do not detect scent particles in the air with the nostrils, as do mammals and most other vertebrates, but by a special structure in the roof of the mouth, called Jacobson's organ, which works together with the tongue. The snake identifies smells from samples of air collected by its tongue each time it flicks it in and out of its mouth, specifically on the ends of the forked tips, and when a snake is hunting or engaged in some other activity, the tongue can often be seen to be moving constantly as the snake strives to gather as much information as possible about its surroundings. So acute is the snake's sense of chemoreception that it can detect even the faintest scent trails left by prey – or another snake. The specialist ant- and termite-hunting blind snakes, for example, can accurately follow an ant trail even a week after the ants have gone.

Sight

In most snakes, vision is quite well developed, but by human standards many are rather short-sighted. Snakes' eyes are different from those of other animals. In humans and most other vertebrates, for example, focusing is achieved with special muscles that change the shape of the lens, whereas in most snakes, there are no such muscles and images are focused instead by the lens moving physically towards or away from the retina. Biologists still know very little about how snakes see, but it seems that essentially their eyes can only detect movement: a snake hunting by sight will often fail to recognize a potential meal unless it begins to move, even if it is only a few centimetres away.

Hearing

Snakes have neither an external ear or an eardrum, although their sense of hearing appears to be otherwise fairly well developed. It is best suited to detecting ground vibrations, thus alerting the snake to approaching danger. These vibrations are picked up from the surface by the bones of the lower jaw and transmitted to the inner ear via a delicate, bony rod (the stapes), in close contact with it. Recent research

BELOW: **Snakes do not have eyelids. Instead the eyes are covered by a transparent protective cap (the brille), as in this Neotropical bird snake,** *Pseustes poecilonotus*; **in some primitive burrowing forms, it is an enlarged and semi-transparent head scale.**

suggests that the ear may be more sensitive to airborne sound than has previously been assumed, and some herpetologists think the lung may play a part in transmitting sound.

Other senses

Rattlesnakes and other other pit vipers, together with most pythons and some boas, are unique among vertebrates in having a highly sophisticated type of sense organ that detects infrared heat and enables them to locate warm-blooded prey (see p. 104). Even more remarkable, the nocturnal olive sea snake (*Aipysurus laevis*) has a series of light-sensitive organs on its tail, which it apparently uses to ensure that the tail is not left exposed (thus revealing its location to a predator) when it is hiding among crevices during the day (see p. 95).

Temperature regulation

Snakes, and reptiles in general, are ectothermic animals that depend almost entirely on external sources of heat and must regulate their body temperatures by behavioural means. To achieve their optimum 'working' temperature they expose themselves to whatever source of heat may be available, such as direct sunlight or a sun-warmed rock. Should they begin to overheat, they cool down by moving into shade, burrowing underground, or immersing themselves in water. They must keep their body temperature within a range of about 4–38°C (39–100°F); if it should fall or rise only a few degrees either side of these levels, they will die.

At times when prevailing conditions make it impossible for snakes to reach or regulate their body temperatures, they escape by hiding away in a state of dormancy. During the freezing conditions of winter in northern Europe, for example, adders (*Vipera berus*) hibernate in underground dens for up to eight months of the year, while in some tropical regions that have long, hot, dry seasons, many snakes will secrete themselves in a cool burrow or beneath the bark of a tree and aestivate to avoid the effects of dehydration.

Despite their reliance on external heat sources and the often cool feel to their bodies when handled, a snake's body temperature can be as high as our own after only a short time basking in the sun, and it is thus misleading to refer to these animals as 'cold-blooded'.

Feeding and diet

Under natural conditions snakes feed more or less exclusively on living prey. A few will occasionally eat carrion (for example, the diet of some North American cottonmouths, *Agkistrodon piscivorus*, includes fish regurgitated by parent seabirds attending nestlings), but this tends to be the exception rather than the rule. Many of the more slender and agile snakes forage actively for prey, while others, such as boas, pythons, and vipers are mostly ambush-hunters that lunge at passing animals from a hiding place. A number of the vipers and several other ambush-hunters have contrastingly coloured tails to lure prey within striking range (see p. 98), and the African twig snake (*Thelotornis capensis*) is said to use its brilliantly coloured red tongue to attract prey in much the same way. The predatory strike of a snake is often too fast to

How snakes move

Precisely how snakes move is one of their most intriguing and mysterious features. Part of the answer lies in their increased number of vertebrae and ribs, which provide the extra flexibility needed for locomotion without limbs. Whereas humans have 32 vertebrae, some species of snakes have over 400. The vertebrae of snakes are among the most elaborate and complicated found in any backboned animals, with a whole range of different structures for supporting the ligaments and tendons that help them move in their characteristic 'slithery' manner.

Most snakes proceed with continuous side to side undulations formed by the natural progression of the body as it follows in line behind the head, where forward movement is achieved by the animal using each of the resulting S-shaped loops to push against irregularities in the ground or obstacles. If the ground over which the snake is moving is unstable, as with loose, shifting sand, or there are no stones, twigs, or other adequate 'footholds' which its body can push against, its ability to move is seriously impaired.

Many of the larger, stouter-bodied snakes, such as pythons, boas, and ground-dwelling vipers, also move by using a rectilinear form of locomotion, whereby they effectively 'walk' on the tips of their ribs in a slow, caterpillar-like crawl. They achieve this by lifting the broad ventral scales upward and forward over the rib tips in successive groups, and then lowering them so that they catch on the ground's surface, where they act as anchors for the snake to pull its body forward. In this way the animal advances in a more or less straight line, albeit rather slowly. Another form of locomotion used by heavy-bodied snakes and also by many burrowing and climbing forms is the 'concertina crawl', in which the animal advances by reaching ahead and pushing its body against the ground, a branch, or some other firm point of anchorage, from where it is then able to pull the rest of its body up behind.

In sandy deserts or other areas where there is no firm ground, several kinds of snakes have developed a modified form of progression known as sidewinding. They throw the body into a succession of S-shaped coils and, instead of the more usual 'slither', take a succession of obliquely-oriented 'steps' over the ground, during which the body is in contact with the surface at only two points at any given moment. The best known exponents of this type of movement are desert-living vipers.

Above: **A horned adder (*Bitis caudalis*) 'sidewinding' over a desert sand dune in Namibia.**

see, and in some species is delivered with such force that much of the body may be thrown forwards.

Swallowing prey

Snakes normally swallow their prey whole, although there are a few instances where they may first discard some body parts; blind snakes, for example, often break off the heads of termites before swallowing them, and white-bellied mangrove snakes (*Fordonia leucobalia*) will twist the legs off a crab if the animal itself is too large to swallow in one piece.

The size of prey eaten by some snakes is truly amazing. Green anacondas (*Eunectes murinus*) and several species of large python are well known for their ability to consume deer, pigs, and occasionally even humans (see p. 40), while small African egg-eating snakes (*Dasypeltis*), with heads scarcely wider than a fingernail, can swallow a hen's egg. Some vipers have been known to ingest meals exceeding 150% of their own body weight. Such incredible feats of swallowing are made possible by the development in many snakes of an enormously distensible and flexible mouth (see p. 8–9). Because they have no sternum (breastbone), the ends of the ribs can also separate widely to allow large prey to pass into the stomach.

DIRECTION: **Spotted python, *Antaresia maculosus*, constricting a rat. Coils thrown around the body of the victim prevent it from inhaling and death is brought about by suffocation.**

swallow large, bulky prey, so with the mouth and throat often completely filled during this period how does it avoid suffocation? The answer is that it can keep its airway open during swallowing because the end of the windpipe (glottis) is strengthened with rings of cartilage, and a further modification enables the glottis to be extended forwards along the floor of the mouth so that breathing can continue unimpeded.

Different diets

Whereas many snakes eat a wide range of prey, others have highly specialized food preferences. Some feed almost exclusively on lizards, birds, or rodents, and there are many that eat nothing but frogs. Among the most unusual dietary specialists are blind snakes, which feed on ants, termites and their pupae, the African egg-eating snakes, snail-eaters, Central American scorpion-eaters, and some sea snakes that eat only fish eggs. Other kinds of prey exploited by specialist feeders include reptile eggs, earthworms, centipedes, bats, crabs, salamanders, amphisbaenians (burrowing snake-like reptiles), and a surprisingly large number of species have a diet that consists chiefly of other snakes.

Some species, such as the Australian taipan (*Oxyuranus scutellatus*) and the black mamba (*Dendroaspis polylepis*) of Africa, live on one or two kinds of prey throughout their entire lives, whereas the food preferences of many others vary according to their age and size, the time of year, or geographical location. Juvenile striped swamp snakes (*Regina alleni*) of North America, for example, always eat shrimp and dragonfly nymphs, whereas adults

Many non-venomous snakes begin swallowing as soon as they have secured a firm grip on their prey, whereas burrowing asps, elapids, vipers and some rear-fanged colubrids first produce paralysis or death in their victim by injecting venom. Others, such as the pythons and boas, first immobilize prey by suffocating it within the coils of their bodies.

A snake usually starts swallowing as soon as it has adjusted its victim into a head-first position. It extends the upper and lower jaws on each side of its head forwards in turn over and around the prey so that, after several repetitions of these movements, the prey is slowly manoeuvred backwards into the throat, eased along during the process by a lubricating coat of saliva. Wave-like contractions of the oesophagus then push the animal down into the snake's stomach. The snake may take up to an hour or more to

ABOVE: **Spotted cat-eyed snake, *Leptodeira septentrionalis*, swallowing a frog. The ability of snakes to swallow large prey is made possible by the development of an enormously distensible mouth and elastic skin.**

feed entirely on crayfish. Water pythons (*Liasis fuscus*) in Australia subsist on flood-plain rats during the dry season and change to a diet of water birds and their eggs in the rainy season (see p. 47), while Mexican parrot snakes (*Leptophis mexicanus*) eat frogs on mainland Central America and mostly lizards on some of the offshore islands.

A well-known feature of snakes is the ability of some species to survive without food for long periods. Pregnant female anacondas in the wild, for example, do not normally eat for the entire six to eight months of gestation, and black tiger snakes (*Notechis ater*) on Mount Chappell Island in the Bass Straight off southern Australia may feed for only a few weeks per year when their principal prey, the chicks of muttonbirds, are available. The record for the longest interval during which a snake has survived without food is held jointly by a green anaconda and an African rock python (*Python sebae*), both of which apparently refused food in captivity for three years before eating again! Under normal circumstances, snakes maintain themselves in continuous state of readiness for feeding, but if food becomes scarce and there are lengthy intervals between meals. the stomachs of some species shrink and their digestive functions revert to a state of temporary suspension.

Venom

According to their principal clinical effects. snake venoms are normally classified as either neurotoxic, attacking nerve tissues and interfering with the transmission of nerve impulses, or haemotoxic, directed towards the blood and circulatory system. Neurotoxic venoms are characteristic mainly of elapid snakes, such as cobras, mambas and coral snakes, bites from which affect the central nervous system and typically lead to death by muscle paralysis and respiratory failure. The haemotoxic venoms of vipers cause tissue destruction, swelling, and blood loss, and death usually results from hypotensive shock as blood pressure drops to a point where the heart can no longer function. Many snake venoms have both neurotoxic and haemotoxic properties. Bites by Neotropical rattlesnakes (*Crotalus durissus*), for example, cause breathing problems as well as symptoms more typical of viper envenomation, while victims of bites from the black-necked spitting cobra (*Naja nigricollis*) often suffer serious local tissue damage.

The toxicity of venom is normally measured by calculating the LD_{50} (50% lethal

BELOW: **A cascabel, *Crotalus durissus*, being 'milked' for the production of snakebite antivenom.**

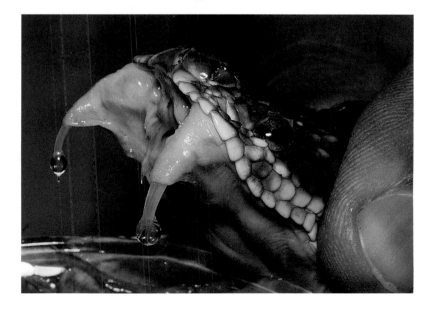

ABOVE: **Eastern green mamba, *Dendroaspis angusticeps*, a member of the elapid family of snakes characterized by the possession of predominantly neurotoxic venoms.**

dose), which is the amount required to kill half of the animals (normally mice) into which it is injected. These provide a general indication of how dangerous the venoms of different snakes may be, but in specific terms they show little correlation with the actual clinical danger of any given species to humans after a bite. Calculations of the LD_{50} value in such snakes as saw-scaled vipers, the bushmaster, kraits, and even the black mamba, for example, look pretty innocuous on paper, whereas researchers know from clinical experience that these are among the most dangerous snakes in existence, with high fatality rates. Furthermore, snake venoms differ considerably in their effect on different animals; the African meerkat, for example, which weighs only about 600 g (21 oz), is, weight-for-weight, one thousand times more resistant to the venom of the Cape cobra (*Naja nivea*) than a sheep! It thus seems clear that the only really useful way of learning about the lethal potential of any snake species

is by studying a good cross-section of clinical cases in humans.

Snake venoms serve two principal purposes: to incapacitate prey and to begin and aid digestion. They consist of various proteins and enzymes and are among the most complex of all biological toxins. More than 30 different enzymes have been identified from snake venoms, although not all of these are found in the venom of any one species. About ten, however, occur in almost all snake venoms. Phospholipase A2 is a particularly widespread enzyme found in the venom of many species, while the venom of stiletto snakes (genus *Atractaspis*) contains a series of unique amino-acid peptides, named sarafotoxins, that have the specific effect of constricting blood vessels and have no known parallel in any other snake venom. Venom composition varies considerably, not just among species, but between populations of the same species, and even within the life of an individual. As juveniles, Brazilian lanceheads *(Bothrops moojeni)*, for example, feed on frogs and lizards, whereas adults eat small mammals, and this change in dietary habits as they grow larger is accompanied by a corresponding increase in venom toxicity.

Various animals that prey on venomous snakes have some degree of natural resistance to their venom. Mongooses are well known for their ability to survive bites from cobras, and the tayra, a Central American member of the weasel family, is able to withstand large doses of terciopelo venom *(Bothrops asper)*. The common mussurana *(Clelia clelia)*, a large colubrid snake from Central and South America, is immune to the venom of pit vipers on which it often feeds, and a recently discovered antitoxic factor in the blood of the reticulated python *(Python reticulatus)*, suggests that this snake is at least partially resistant to the bite of Russell's viper *(Daboia russelli)*.

Snake venoms are routinely collected for the production of antivenoms, and their potential medical applications have increasingly become the subject of high-investment research. Captotril (Capoten), a multi-million-dollar drug recently developed for treating high blood pressure, for example, is based on a component originally found in the venom of the jararaca *(Bothrops jararaca)*, a South American pit viper.

Reproduction

Most snakes are oviparous, reproducing by laying eggs, although approximately a quarter of all species are viviparous, giving birth to fully-formed young. Sometimes, both kinds of

BELOW: **Vipers, such as the dusky lancehead,** *Bothrops pulcher*, **typically have venoms that are haemotoxic in nature.**

reproduction occur within a single species in different parts of its range. In most snakes males are more abundant than females, but there are at least two species in which the entire population appears to consist only of females. These extraordinary snakes reproduce without males by means of parthenogenesis ('virgin birth'), and the young snakes are born as miniature clones of their mothers (see p. 31).

Courtship

In almost all snakes there is a pattern of courtship that precedes mating, and while details vary between different species, it tends on the whole to involve the same general sequence of events. The male, which is almost always the active partner, first searches out a receptive female by following the scent trail that she produces from special anal glands as she moves around. Once he has located her,

he approaches and proceeds to work his way gradually forwards over her body with rapid, quivering movements, at the same time rubbing his chin along her back and flicking his tongue in and out constantly. In many of the pythons and boas the male uses the claw-like vestiges of his hind limbs to scratch or stroke the female's skin, which appears to have the same stimulative effect. When he reaches the nape of her neck, the male then manoeuvres himself into a mating position by throwing a loop of his body over the lower part of her back and entwining his tail around her cloaca (the common opening of the reproductive and digestive tract). If the female is receptive, she responds by raising her tail slightly and opening her cloaca; then the male everts one of his paired hemipenes and copulates with her.

Mating is usually a protracted affair, and the male and female may remain joined

BELOW: **A copulating pair of amethystine or giant scrub pythons,** *Morelia amethystinus*, **Queensland, Australia.**

together for many hours. In some species, the female may be surrounded by considerable numbers of males, which in their impassioned attempts to mate with her and 'squeeze' out competing rivals will often entwine themselves together in a large jumbled mass. Herpetologists have observed this 'balling' behaviour in various different snakes, especially aquatic forms such as anacondas, green water snakes (*Nerodia cyclopion*), Arafura file snakes (*Acrochrodus arafurae*), and some sea snakes. A breeding ball of anacondas may consist of 2-12 males, all coiled around a single female, and they will stay knotted together like this for up to four weeks. Fertilization may not necessarily happen straight away after mating. Sperm can survive in the female reproductive tract for long periods, and there are instances where the females of some species in captivity have been kept away from males for several years and then unexpectedly given birth to healthy offspring.

Ritualistic combat

Should they encounter each other during the breeding season, the males of many species become aggressive and perform ritualistic combat 'dances'. These competitions take place between adult males of the same species, and usually between individuals that are similarly matched in size. When two such rivals meet, they rise up vertically against each other and entwine their bodies like a twisted rope, each attempting to dominate the other by pushing him over. The display is frequently accompanied by exaggerated swaying movements as each snake attempts to knock the other off balance, and finally ends when the weaker opponent concedes by dropping to the ground and hastily moving away.

Ritualistic combat dances have been observed in species as widely different as American indigo snakes (*Drymarchon corais*), European vipers (*Vipera*), black mambas (*Dendroaspis polylepis*) in Africa, and Australian tiger snakes (*Notechis*). Essentially, they amount to little more than a vigorous test of strength, and except in a few species in which a frustrated male may bite his rival, neither snake usually inflicts serious injury on the other. So preoccupied can a male become in his battle for supremacy that he may become completely oblivious to what is happening around him; a male European adder (*Vipera berus*), for example, will sometimes continue to 'dance' in this way even when its rival has been removed and replaced with a stick!

Eggs and hatching

Eggs are usually laid several weeks or months after mating, and vary greatly in number according to species and, in many cases, the size of the parent female. Most of the smaller kinds of snakes, such as blind snakes and some invertebrate-eating members of the Colubridae, typically produce only two or three eggs that in comparison with their body sizes are enormous, while large pythons may lay up to 100 relatively small eggs. Viviparous species in particular often give birth to large numbers of offspring; the record is held by a puff adder (*Bitis arietans*), which produced 156 young in a single litter.

The female snake usually deposits her eggs underground or in a shallow hole on the surface covered with leaves, where they are concealed from predators and insulated from fluctuations in temperature and humidity. The incubation temperature and moisture level to which the eggs are exposed have a direct bearing on their development, and it is thus vitally important that she selects her nest site very carefully; a temperature increase of only a few degrees can halve the time required for the eggs to hatch, while if the nest area becomes too hot or does not retain enough heat, the developing embryos within the eggs will perish. In a particularly suitable place, females may deposit their eggs communally and even return to the same site year after year. Favourite nesting sites of the grass snake (*Natrix natrix*) in Britain, for example, are garden compost heaps; as these decompose, they generate a good deal of heat, providing an ideal environment for incubation.

Although most snakes leave the nest site and have nothing further to do with the eggs once they are laid, the females of certain kinds, notably pythons and a number of tropical vipers, remain with their clutch during the entire incubation period. Female pythons are unusual in also being able to control the temperature at which their eggs develop (see p. 38). The time that elapses before the eggs hatch varies greatly among species; in some blind snakes hatching may occur only a few days after the eggs have been laid, while in others it may take more than three months. At hatching time, the young snakes break through the leathery shell using a small egg-tooth attached to the end of their snouts, which is discarded shortly afterwards. The young of live-bearing snakes are born enclosed within a membranous sac, which ruptures soon after birth.

Predator evasion and defence

Snakes show a wide range of behaviour in response to predators, and the defensive repertoires of some species are elaborate. Almost invariably, however, a snake's first reaction when confronted with danger is to try to escape observation, either by remaining

BELOW: Snakes that rely on immobility to evade detection have complex colour patterns that serve to break up the outline of the body and often resemble dead leaves, moss, bark etc. Eyelash palm pit viper (*Bothriechis schlegelii*), Costa Rica.

Colubridae are distinctive in having long, thin bodies that resemble vines, and some, such as those of the genus *Oxybelis*, also have the habit of moving with an irregular swaying action, mimicking a vine or branch trembling in the breeze.

Warning colouration

In contrast to colour patterns that provide concealment, those of some snakes are designed to purposely solicit attention and warn predators of their owners' harmful character. Aposematic (warning) colour patterns, as they are known, are exhibited also by a number of mostly harmless 'mimic' species, which derive protection from them in much the same way (see p. 81).

ABOVE: Coral snakes have bright colour patterns that appear to be instinctively avoided by many predators. Similar markings are seen also in a number of harmless 'mimic' species; compare this Maya coral snake, *Micrurus hippocrepis*, with the false coral snake (below).

BELOW: False coral snakes, *Urotheca elapoides*, have exceptionally long, fragile tails, which are easily broken and thus provide the snake with more than one chance of escape.

motionless or withdrawing discreetly out of sight. Most species are coloured and patterned in a way that conceals them in their natural habitat, reducing the risk of detection by predators and helping them stay hidden from potential prey; this is known as procrypsis. The complex geometrical markings of Gaboon vipers (*Bitis gabonica*), for example, are extremely effective in disguising these huge African snakes among fallen leaves on the forest floor, while the mottled green patterns of some palm pit vipers (*Bothriechis*) are perhaps unsurpassed in concealing these species among the greenery of tropical American rainforests. A number of tree-living specialists in the

Escape

Should their initial attempts to avoid discovery fail, most snakes will try to make good their escape by fleeing. Many of the long, slender terrestrial species in particular are highly agile and when confronted with danger will disappear with a burst of great speed; a startled pink-tailed forest racer (*Dendrophidion nuchale*), for example, will dash across the forest floor for 20 m (65 ft) or more before stopping, and these whip-like Central American snakes may also escape by flinging themselves spectacularly off high rocky outcrops. The paradise tree snakes (*Chrysopelea*) of India and Southeast Asia have an even more impressive way of avoiding danger. Also known as 'flying' snakes, these accomplished climbers will throw themselves off the highest branches and, with their bodies flattened, glide down to the ground or a lower branch.

Tail breakage

The ability of a species to voluntarily cast off its tail (autotomy) to escape a predator is most commonly associated with lizards, but there are also several snakes in which this extraordinary behaviour has arisen. Whereas the broken tail of many lizards will grow back however, snakes cannot regenerate their tails. The mechanism of tail breakage in snakes is also different from that in lizards; in most lizards the break occurs directly across a vertebral segment, whereas in snakes it occurs between the vertebrae. In some snakes tail loss is limited to a single breakage, with no further breaks occurring after the initial one, whereas the mechanism in others, such as the neck-banded snake (*Scaphiodontophis annulatus*) and the harlequin snake (*Urotheca elapoides*) of Central America appears more specialized.

Intimidation displays

Many snakes resort to hissing when confronted with danger, and various species are known to use other sounds as a means of discouraging unwanted attention. The audible threat displays of rattlesnakes produced by the rapid vibration of their tail rattles are particularly intimidating. Neotropical lanceheads (*Bothrops*) do not have rattles, but many of these species and several others are able to generate similar sound effects by vibrating their tails among dry leaves. Saw-scaled vipers (*Echis*) and desert horned vipers (*Cerastes cerastes*) produce a rasping sound by rubbing their coarsely-keeled body scales together, while Western hook-nosed snakes

RIGHT: **Should their initial escape attempts fail, many snakes resort to intimidation tactics when confronted with danger. The startle and threat display of the Asian lined rat snake, *Elaphe radiata*, is particularly demonstrative.**

LEFT: **Cobras are noted for their upright hooded threat posture. The forest cobra (*Naja melanoleuca*) is a particularly large African species that can rear to a great height – over two-thirds of its body may be raised from the ground.**

(*Gyalopion canum*) and Sonoran coral snakes (*Micruroides euryxanthus*) are noted for the curious 'popping' sounds they make by drawing air in though the cloaca and expelling it under force.

Some tree-dwelling snakes, including Neotropical bird snakes (*Pseustes*), the Australian tree snake (*Dendrelaphis punctulatus*), and the African twig snakes (*Thelotornis*) and boomslang (*Dispholidus typus*), respond to threats by expanding the neck to appear larger than life. Many snakes also open their mouths wide when alarmed, and some, such as the brown vine snake (*Oxybelis aeneus*) from Central America, reveal a strikingly contrasting colour when they open their mouths.

Passive resistance

When other lines of defence have all been exhausted and they have no further strategy to fall back on, some snakes resort to various passive forms of behaviour. Several roll themselves into balls, and some will try to confuse an enemy further by raising and waving their short stumpy tails to imitate a moving head; to add to the illusion, the tails of some species are patterned to resemble the head. Asian sand boas (*Eryx tataricus*), for example, have tail markings that consist of a short, dark horizontal line and a small spot, resembling the mouth and eye.

Another odd form of passive resistance is that used by, among others, the North American hognosed snakes (*Heterodon*). When molested, these snakes turn over onto their backs and, after a few convulsive wriggles, lie still with their mouths open and tongues hanging out, pretending to be dead; if the 'lifeless' snake is turned over onto its belly again, however, it gives the game away by promptly rolling back. Even more remarkable is the autohaemorrhaging behaviour of wood snakes (*Tropidophis*) (see p. 53).

As a further deterrent, some Asian keelbacks (*Macropisthodon* and some species of *Rhabdophis*) produce a sticky, bitter-tasting substance from neck glands when provoked, and many other snakes will smear themselves with either obnoxious secretions from musk glands at the base of the tail or the contents of their cloacas. These can be especially foul-smelling and the odour often persists for many hours, as anyone who has caught a grass snake or garter snake will not have failed to notice!

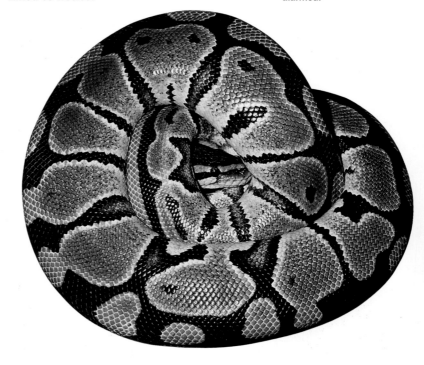

BELOW: **Royal pythons,** *Python regius*, **are among a number of species that habitually roll themselves up into a tight ball when alarmed.**

Primitive Burrowing Snakes

Having almost certainly evolved from ancestors rather similar to modern-day lizards, the most primitive kinds of snakes alive today tend to be those that have retained the most lizard-like features. Blind snakes, pipe snakes and several other clearly recognizable groups fall into this category, most of which include small species that are partly, if not entirely, adapted for an underground life (exceptions include pythons and boas).

All these burrowing species have a stout, rather inflexible skull with a coronoid bone (a small bone in the lower jaw retained in primitive snakes but lost in more advanced families: see p. 9), eyes that are somewhat degenerate in form, smooth scales that look as if they have been polished, and two lungs (or the absence of a tracheal lung). Except for

BELOW: *Typhlops angolenesis*, a large blind snake found throughout much of tropical Africa.

one group, the shieldtails (family Uropeltidae), they also have a pelvic girdle – and, in most cases, also vestigial hind limbs. Unlike those of most other snakes, the ventral scales are either undifferentiated or only slightly wider than the dorsal ones. This condition is also found in some advanced snakes, such as the true sea snakes (family Elapidae), but in this group it is clear that their absence is a secondary loss – broad ventral scales are a useful adaptation for locomotion on land, but are not needed for swimming.

Blind snakes
Families *Leptotyphlopidae*, *Typhlopidae* and *Anomalepididae*

Three families of small, primitive snakes, to which the name 'blind snake' is often collectively applied, are among the most distinctive of all living serpents. So peculiar is their appearance it is difficult to appreciate that they belong to the same group of vertebrates as, for example, the huge pythons, and it was once even suggested that they are not snakes at all. Although they are perhaps not totally blind, the eyes of most species are very reduced in size and appear capable of distinguishing only between light and dark. Each eye is not covered by its own, circular protective cap (the brille), as in most other snakes, but usually lies beneath an enlarged scale on the side of the head. The seven-striped

LEFT: *Typhlops congestus*, a large species of Central African forests that may grow up to 1 m (3.3 ft).

blind snake (*Leptotyphlops septemstriatus*) has a distinct pupil and coloured iris, and may have better developed vision, but a few species lack eyes altogether.

Some blind snakes are the smallest of all snakes. An African species, Schlegel's blind snake (*Rhinotyphlops schlegelii*) is unusual in that it grows to almost 1 m (3 ft) long and about 5 cm (2 in) in diameter, although in general the average length of these curious little snakes is 15–30 cm (6–12 in). Some of the smallest species are little more than 10 cm (4 in) long as adults and only 2 mm (0.08 in) across. They have small, bluntly rounded heads with bizarrely-shaped skulls. The lower jaws are somewhat recessed and, unlike those of most other snakes, rigidly attached to each other at the front. Some species have teeth only on the upper or lower jaw. Their worm-like bodies are long, narrow, and cylindrical, and covered with smooth, strongly overlapping scales of the same general shape

throughout. *Ramphotyphlops angusticeps* from the Solomon Islands has a particularly long body with more than 600 individual vertebrae, perhaps the greatest number of any snake and certainly more than any other vertebrate. The tail is always very short, as little as 1% of the total length in some species, and capped at its tip with a tiny sharp spine. As a further adaptation for burrowing, the rostral scale on the snout is enlarged for pushing through loose earth, and there are often many small glands on the head, whose precise function is not clear.

BELOW: **Skull of thread snake. Leptotyphlopids are unique among snakes in that all of the bones of the upper jaw and palate have lost their teeth. Note the long lower bone (quadrate) for pushing the small mouth outwards.**

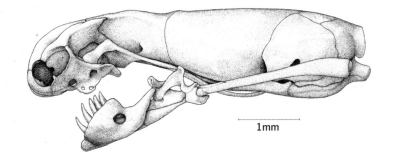

1mm

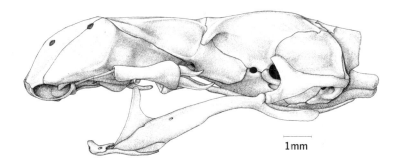

1mm

The family Leptotyphlopidae, commonly known as slender blind snakes or thread snakes in allusion to their very elongated, narrow bodies, includes about 60 species distributed throughout the warmer parts of the world. Except for *Rhinoleptus koniagui* of western Africa, the sole member of the genus *Rhinoleptus*, all are placed in the genus *Leptotyphlops*.

About 220 species in the family Typhlopidae, distributed among six genera, bear a strong superficial resemblance to the slender blind snakes but have more rows of scales around the body. These species also have no enlarged scale covering the vent.

The Anomalepidae includes only about 16 species in four genera (*Anomalepis, Helminthophis, Liotyphlops, Typhlophis*), restricted in distribution to tropical Central and South America. In evolutionary terms, these snakes seem more advanced than other blind snakes and differ from them in lacking vestiges of a pelvis and several other features of the skeleton. The lower jaw is also longer and more flexible, with teeth usually on both upper and lower jaws.

Many blind snakes are uniform in colour, often a pale and somewhat translucent pink,

ABOVE: **Skull of blind snake. The upper jaw usually has at least a few teeth, while the lower is toothless; unlike leptotyphlopids the maxillary bones of the upper jaw are also not rigidly attached to each other but capable of some independent movement.**

BELOW: *Ramphotyphlops nigrescens* **from Australia.**

but others are entirely black or brown. Some of these darker forms have contrasting pale heads and tails, while some Amazonian species of *Leptotyphlops* are marked with prominent dorsal stripes of black and red or yellow. They occur in all the warmer parts of the world, in habitats as diverse as deserts, grasslands and tropical rainforests.

Feeding and reproduction

Blind snakes have a specialist diet that consists mostly of ants, termites, and their larvae and pupae, and many of them are regular co-habitants of ant and termite nests. Even the largest species appear to feed almost exclusively on invertebrates, and may eat large numbers of them. The snake usually eats only the ant's soft-bodied abdomen; once it has swallowed this, it breaks off the hard chitinous head by pressing it against the ground. *Acutotyphlops subocularis* of New Guinea is one of a few species that are unusual in that they feed mostly on

Blind snakes and screech-owls

Eastern screech-owls (*Otus asio*) feed mainly on insects, but among the various other small animals that parent birds in southern USA occasionally catch and take back to their nestlings are Texas blind snakes (*Leptotyphlops dulcis*). Unusually, however, the owls do not always kill the snakes, as they do most other kinds of prey, but carry them back to the nest alive, where apparently many are then released (or escape from the bird's bill and talons) and survive by eating the larvae of parasitic insects. Some captured snakes continue to live in the nest, feeding on the larvae even after the young owls have fledged.

Infestations of scavenging and parasitic insects often plague the nests of screech-owls, and this appears to be one of the main underlying reasons why in parts of their range their broods so often fail. Young owls in nests that contain blind snakes, however, appear to grow faster and suffer lower mortality than do those in which there are no snakes, so evidently there is at least some benefit to the owls in having these live-in cleaners around. It remains to be seen if the occurrence of blind snakes in screech-owl nests is merely the result of them having fortuitously escaped being eaten, or if there is some complex, mutually beneficial interaction between these animals at play. Where they occur in other parts of the world, blind snakes are often preyed on by owls and invariably eaten by these birds.

LEFT: **Texas blind snake,** *Leptotyphlops dulcis.*

earthworms, which are swallowed whole. While feeding, many species smother themselves with a distasteful secretion to repel attacking ants. Texas blind snakes (*Leptotyphlops dulcis*), and perhaps other species too, also form a physical barrier against the bites of these insects by raising the tips of their body scales.

All blind snakes are probably egg-layers, and except for some anomalepids have only one oviduct, perhaps an evolutionary consequence of their slender body shape. Clutch size ranges from a single, long and very narrow – 25 x 2.5 mm (1 x 0.1 in) – egg in Asian *Leptotyphlops blanfordii*, to as many as 60, each about 20 x 10 mm (0.8–0.4 in), in the giant Schlegel's blind snake. The eggs laid by some species are so tiny that in size and shape they resemble a grain of rice. Some species lay eggs that are in a very advanced stage of development and hatch within a few days.

Among the most unusual of the blind snakes in its reproductive biology is the Brahminy blind snake, *Rhamphotyphlops braminus*, which is believed to be an all-female, parthenogenetic species (that is, it produces offspring without males). This species is also called the 'flower-pot snake' because of its tendency to hide in the soil of potted plants, by which means it has been accidentally transported by humans to many places. A native of southern Asia, it has now become established in regions as far apart as Madagascar, Japan, Australia, Hawaii, Mexico and southeastern USA.

Pipe snakes
Families *Aniliidae, Cylindrophiidae* and *Anomochilidae*

These snakes have long, cylindrical bodies and ventral scales that are either undifferentiated or only slightly wider than the dorsal ones. The Aniliidae comprises a single species, *Anilius scytale*, found in the forests of Amazonian South America while the Cylindrophiidae is represented by ten Asian and Indonesian species grouped in the genus *Cylindrophis*. Sometimes included within the Cylindrophiidae, the single genus and two species of the family Anomochilidae are restricted to peninsular Malaysia and parts of Indonesia.

Pipe snakes feed on other snakes, caecilians (burrowing, legless amphibians), amphisbaenians (burrowing, legless lizards), and infant rodents in their nests, while *Anilius* and some Asian species also eat eels. The diets of *Anomochilus* are unknown, but the small head and body size of these odd little snakes indicate that they may eat only small caecilians, newborn snakes, or perhaps worms and other invertebrates.

The South American false coral pipe snake (*Anilius scytale*) has very small eyes that lie beneath a relatively large, transparent, polygonal scale. This species also retains the primitive feature of teeth on the premaxilla (see p. 9). Although mostly burrowing in habit, it is also commonly found in water. It gives birth to 3–13 young.

Asian pipe snakes (family Cylindrophiidae) have conspicuously flattened tails which, when danger threatens, they curl upwards to expose red- or orange-mottled undersurfaces. The dorsal colour of some species is uniform brown, while others are marked with black cross-bars and a lengthways stripe along the middle of the back, and all species have black-and-white-chequered abdomens. Like other pipe snakes, they are burrowers in loose, wet soil or leaf litter, usually close to the surface. They are all live-bearers.

BELOW: **Skull of pipe snake. Pipe snakes have a primitive skull structure with only a few large teeth. The snout and jaw bones are not movably connected to each other or the braincase, as in more advanced snakes, and the lower jaw, too, is relatively inflexible.**

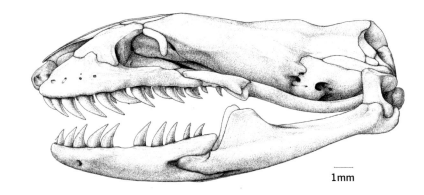

1mm

31

Dwarf pipe snakes (*Anomochilus*) are small species, growing to only just over 40 cm (16 in). They are boldly marked with yellow or white spots, and at least one species has red bands on the tail. Unlike other pipe snakes, they are egg-layers, although apart from this very little is known about their natural history. *Anomochilus weberi*, a very rare species from Sumatra and Kalimantan, appears to live in rainforests.

BELOW: **The strikingly marked South American pipe snake, *Anilius scytale*, is about 90 cm (3 ft) long when fully grown.**

Shieldtailed snakes
Family *Uropeltidae*

The shieldtails, of which there are eight genera (*Brachyophidium, Melanophidium, Platyplectrurus, Plectrurus, Pseudotyphlops, Rhinophis, Teretrurus, Uropeltis*) and 47 species, are a group of distinctive-looking snakes restricted to the Indian subcontinent and Sri Lanka. They resemble pipe snakes in having a primitive type of skull that is especially stout and robust, although differ from these species in having no vestiges of the hind limbs or a pelvis, and are also more radically modified for subterranean life.

Among their various burrowing adaptations is a unique feature that affects the mobility of the head. The first two vertebrae of the neck have exceptionally flexible joints, allowing the snake to bend its head to an unusually sharp angle; the muscles of the neck and forepart of the body have also become especially well developed for pushing the narrow, pointed head forcefully through soil. When tunnelling, the neck makes a series of regular sideways-directed movements, which widens the burrow through which the snake is moving and allows it to draw the rest of its body up behind.

LEFT: **Asian pipe snakes range in length from about 40 cm (16 in) in the Sri Lankan pipe snake (*Cylindrophis maculatus*) to 70 cm (28 in) in this species, the red-tailed pipe snake (*C. ruffus*).**

The most notable feature of shieldtails, and the feature for which they are collectively named, is the oddly shaped end of the tail. In some species this is capped with a spine or has an enlarged, roughened scale, while in others the tail terminates abruptly as a broad, flattened disk covered with spiny protuberances. Internally, the tip of the tail is supported by a bony plate. The curiously modified tails of these snakes probably serve some adaptive function in protecting them; when threatened with attack, a shieldtail will tuck its head between the body coils and wave its tail around, a behavioural trait that probably evolved as a means of diverting a predator's attention away from the snake's more vulnerable head.

Shieldtails are small snakes, about 20–75 cm (8–30 in) in length. Some species are brilliantly coloured, with red, orange, or yellow markings, while others are uniformly black. Their scales are often highly iridescent. They occur mostly in mountain rainforests, although some, such as the monotypic *Pseudotyphlops philippinus* of Sri Lanka, are now also apparently common in lowland agricultural areas. They feed mainly on earthworms, and while burrowing in search of prey often form deep underground tunnels. Some species occasionally congregate in small colonies.

Sunbeam Snakes
Families *Loxocemidae* and *Xenopeltidae*

The Loxocemidae and Xenopeltidae are enigmatic families that share an assortment of both primitive and advanced features, and may be closely related. Their scales have an unusually iridescent quality, particularly those of the Asian *Xenopeltis unicolor*, and for this reason they are often referred to as 'sunbeam snakes'. They are essentially burrowing snakes of moderate size – about 1 m (3 ft) in length – and are all egg-layers.

Loxocemus bicolor from the New World tropics (Neotropics) is the sole living representative of the Loxocemidae. It was long considered a relative of the pythons, and has been also variously linked with the pipe snakes of the Family Aniliidae as well as with the Xenopeltidae. It has vestiges of a pelvic girdle, and also the primitive features of paired lungs, a postfrontal bone, and premaxillary teeth. The true affinities of this curious snake remain unclear, although they probably lie most closely with the Xenopeltidae.

Loxocemus is a semi-burrowing species; it is a constrictor and feeds on lizards and small rodents, largely underground. Turtle and iguana eggs also feature in its diet. Originally described from El Salvador, it occurs in Mexico and the Pacific lowlands of Central America.

The Xenopeltidae is an Old World family with one genus, *Xenopeltis*, and two species, both in Asia. In general appearance they resemble *Loxocemus*, especially in body proportions and the appearance of their scales, and like this species have a pair of lungs, premaxillary teeth, and a jaw mechanism that is more flexible than that of pipe snakes and other primitive groups. They are also largely subterranean in habit. Unlike *Loxocemus*, however, there is no postfrontal bone or evidence of a pelvic girdle. Asian sunbeam snakes have a rather cylindrical body, and for burrowing the head is quite flattened and shovel-shaped. Their eyes are rather small. They also have a very flexible lower jaw for grasping the hard-scaled bodies of skinks, which are their main prey. They also eat small mammals, frogs, and other snakes. *Xenopeltis unicolor*, the most wide-ranging species, lives in India, southern China, and throughout much of Southeast Asia, including many of the Indonesian and Philippine islands. Its less well-known relative, *X. hainanensis*, appears to occur only in China.

OPPOSITE: **Neotropical sunbeam snake,** *Loxocemus bicolor.*

BELOW: **Asian sunbeam snake,** *Xenopeltis unicolor.* **The smooth, polished scales of sunbeam snakes help reduce friction when burrowing or moving through dense vegetation.**

Boas and Pythons
Family *Boidae*

By virtue of their legendary size, pythons and boas must rank among the most familiar of all vertebrate animals. While a number of species do reach enormous lengths, however, the family also includes a number of small, specialized forms that grow to little more than 1 m (3 ft).

Boas and pythons represent an ancient group. Primitive features found in all species are a long row of palatal teeth and a pelvis with vestigial hind limbs, visible as small claw-like spurs at the base of the tail. Most have a functional left lung, and some also have postfrontal bones, premaxillary teeth, and small pits in the labial scales associated with temperature-sensing (see p. 38, 104).

OPPOSITE: **Children's python, *Antaresia childreni*. The females of many python species brood their eggs for up to 3 months or more, during which time they do not feed and may leave only occasionally to bask or drink.**

BELOW: **Macklot's python, *Liasis mackloti*, a large semi-aquatic species from Indonesia, Papua New Guinea, and coastal northern Australia.**

The bones of the skull are more loosely articulated than in the burrowing and other primitive snakes, enabling boas and pythons to swallow particularly large prey. Anyone who has observed these snakes feeding cannot fail to be impressed by their extraordinary ability to extend the jaws around what often seems to be an impossibly large mouthful.

Affinities of boas and pythons

Boas and pythons resemble each other in many features, especially in their adaptations to similar environmental conditions, and many herpetologists think they have both arisen from the same recent ancestor. However, these two groups of snakes are almost completely mutually exclusive in their geographic distribution. There are no boas in Southeast Asia or Australia, only pythons, of which there are eight species in the former region and 20 in the latter. In the Americas and Madagascar, there are only boas (21 species in the former and three in the latter). Only in the New Guinea region and parts of India and Africa do the ranges of some species overlap, and in these areas they tend to occupy different habitats. Based in part on these different distributions and also on thorough analyses of their physical characteristics, most researchers now accept that boas and pythons are not as closely related as was once believed, and even that they may be better divided into separate families.

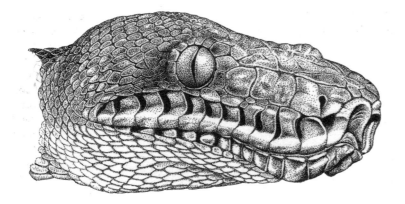

ABOVE: **Where present, the heat sensory organs of boas occur between the labial (lip) scales, as exhibited by the emerald tree boa (top); those of pythons (such as this amethystine python) are placed within the scales.**

muscles, which has the effect of considerably increasing the temperature between the female's body and the eggs around which she is coiled. When the ambient air temperature is too low, the female envelops the clutch more tightly within her coils and increases the rate of contractions, or 'twitching', while if it is too high, she relaxes her body to permit greater ventilation, and twitches less frequently. A female python may stay coiled around her eggs for the entire incubation period (up to three months or more in some species), leaving them only occasionally to drink or bask.

True boas
Subfamily *Boinae*

Boa constrictors and anacondas

Four species of large boas (*Boa*) include one of the most familiar of all the snakes in this group, the common boa constrictor (*B. constrictor*). This tropical American species has one of the largest geographic distributions of any boid, ranging from Mexico in the north and throughout Central and northern South America into Argentina, and it also occurs in a wide variety of habitats. Common boas are large and heavy-bodied, and although they were long believed to have reached a length of 5.6 m (18.5 ft), they rarely seem to grow larger than 3.6 m (12 ft).

Also included in the genus *Boa* are three species from Madagascar. The Madagascan ground boa (*Boa dumerili*) and Dumeril's ground boa (*B. madagascariensis*) are heavy-bodied terrestrial species that attain lengths

The 26 species of pythons are distinguished from boas in the arrangement of certain bones of the skull, the placement of their heat-detecting pits and, except for one Australian genus, in having teeth on the premaxilla. Pythons also lay eggs, whereas boas typically give birth to fully-formed live young. The females of many pythons are able to incubate their eggs using muscular contractions of the body to generate heat – an unexpected ability for an animal that is otherwise regarded as 'cold-blooded' and incapable of producing metabolic heat. This is achieved by spasmodic contractions of the

LEFT: Dumeril's ground boa, *Boa dumerili*, is one of three boa species restricted to Madagascar whose nearest relative is *Boa constrictor* of tropical America. These species have probably all evolved from a common ancestor that lived at the time when Madagascar and the Americas were joined together.

of approximately 2 m (6.5 ft), while *B. manditra* is a slightly smaller and more slender tree-dweller.

Another famous group of boas are the anacondas (*Eunectes*) of which the green anaconda (*E. murinus*) is arguably the largest snake in the world (see p. 40). This truly enormous species has a wide distribution over much of tropical South America. A smaller species, the yellow anaconda, *E. notaeus*, occurs in southern parts of the Amazon basin and one other species, *E. deschauenseei*, lives on the island of Marajó in the mouth of the Amazon. Anacondas are highly aquatic boas in which the eyes and nostrils are on top of the head, and they are almost always found in or near to water, especially swamps and slow-moving rivers. They are mostly ambush hunters and feed on a wide range of prey. In the seasonally flooded llanos (grassy plains) of Venezuela, green anacondas conceal themselves beneath dense floating mats of water hyacinth, from where they lunge at prey as large as the sheep-sized capybaras and occasionally small caimans.

LEFT: Common boas (*Boa constrictor*) are among the largest snakes in tropical America, although even large specimens, such as this 3 m (10 ft) long example at the side of a forest track, are not easy to see.

Giant snakes

*'There lay in the mud and water, covered
with flies, butterflies and insects of all
sorts, the most colossal anaconda which
ever my wildest dreams had conjured up.
Ten or twelve feet of it lay stretched out on
the bank in the mud. The rest of it lay in
the clear, shallow water, one huge loop of it
under our canoe, its body as thick as a
man's waist. It measured fifty feet for
certainty, and probably nearer sixty'.*

So wrote an explorer (F.W. Up de Graff, in
Head Hunters of the Amazon, 1923) of an
encounter in Amazonian Ecuador with a
monster anaconda. Although possibly not
the longest snake in the world, the green
anaconda (*Eunectes murinus*) is certainly
the most massive, sometimes exceeding
0.9 m (3 ft) in circumference and over
205 kg (450 lb) in weight. Whether or not
these snakes grow to some of the
gargantuan sizes claimed is, however, the
subject of much controversy. Most early
references to 'giant' anacondas and pythons
appear to have been grossly exaggerated or
based on the length of the removed skin,
which is easily stretched. The longest
known anaconda, found in the upper
Orinoco River of eastern Colombia during
the 1930s, is believed to have been 11.4 m
(37.5 ft) long, although many herpetologists
remain sceptical about this record and
consider the maximum size attained by
these snakes as nearer 9 m (30 ft).

Another infamous 'giant' is the
reticulated python (*Python reticulatus*) of
Southeast Asia. This species is also claimed
to attain lengths of 9 m (30 ft) or more,
though it does not rival the sheer girth and
bulk of its South American relative. The
largest known specimen, from Sulawesi, is
understood to have measured 10 m (33 ft).
Probably the most reliable documented
length for a reticulated python is for an
individual appropriately named 'Colossus',
that lived for many years at the Pittsburgh
Zoo; it measured 8.7 m (28.5 ft) and
weighed 145 kg (320 lb).

Almost as controversial as the size
attained by anacondas and the larger
species of python are tales about what they
reputedly eat. In parts of South America,
for example, anacondas are often held
responsible for the unexplained
disappearance of horses and oxen, and in
Africa, large rock pythons (*Python sebae*)
are believed by some to prey on buffalo. In
1952 a Sri Lankan newspaper even carried
an article describing a python (presumably
Python molurus) attacking a baby elephant.
While such stories seem outrageous, and
are probably based on little more than
hearsay and fabrication, these snakes are
nonetheless capable of consuming
enormous meals. One genuine case
concerns an 5.5 m (18 ft) Asian rock
python which, having been discovered with
a huge bulge in its stomach, was found to
have eaten a full-grown leopard.

BELOW: **Green anaconda,
Eunectes murinus, at Ilha
Caviana on the Amazon
River, Brazil.**

Tree boas

Seven species of tree boas (genus *Corallus*) are a specialized group of tree-dwellers with relatively slender bodies flattened from side to side, long prehensile tails, and very long mandibular teeth. The common tree boa genus has four species, two of which (*C. hortulanus* and *C. ruschenbergerii*) occur on the South American mainland, with the others on the Caribbean islands of St. Vincent (*C. cookii*), and Grenada (*C. grenadensis*).

Cropani's boa, *C. cropanii*, is one of the rarest snakes in the world (see p. 42).

Tree boas are nocturnal snakes that use both active and ambush hunting methods to catch their prey. In terms of food preferences, the least specialized is the common tree boa (*C. hortulanus*), which eats frogs, lizards, birds, and small mammals, including bats. Emerald tree boas (*C. canina*) and annulated tree boas (*C. annulatus*) are relatively stout-bodied snakes that show a strong preference

ABOVE: **A new-born emerald tree boa, *Corallus canina*. As these snakes mature their colour pattern gradually changes to bright green (see p. 50).**

ABOVE: **Cropani's boa,** *Corallus cropani*.

An endangered rarity

Snakes may be rare in the wild for a variety of reasons. Their numbers may be affected, for example, by habitat destruction, exploitation by the leather and pet animal trades, or through their use as food, but some species seem to have always been extremely scarce even in pristine, undisturbed habitat. Among these is Cropani's boa (*C. cropanii*) which is represented by perhaps no more than three specimens in museum collections, all of which have originated from the vicinity of the type locality (the site from which

the original specimen was described) near Miracatu in the State of São Paulo, Brazil. Virtually nothing is known about its natural history other than that it occurs in the Atlantic rainforests at 40–45 m (130–150 ft) above sea level. Herpetologists do not know why it is so rare. Although restricted to a much diminished habitat, there is still a good deal of intact and protected Atlantic forest remaining in São Paulo State, particularly in the general region where the specimens of *C. cropanii* have been found, and given the level of encroachment on the area during forest clearance and agricultural work it is rather surprising that more specimens have not come to light.

There is also a long history of local people in Brazil, and especially São Paulo State, bringing any snakes encountered to the Instituto Butantan research centre in São Paulo, and even today this institute receives thousands of snakes from the general range of Cropani's boa every year, including many from plots being cleared and areas of virgin forest. Despite this, however, no further specimens have been brought in, and whether or not this elusive boa still survives remains a mystery.

LEFT: **Black-tailed tree boa,** *Corallus ruschenbergerii*, **a species from Costa Rica, Panama, and northern South America.**

for rodents and other endothermic prey. Where prey is abundant, Granada tree boas in particular may be relatively common. Some of the densest populations of this species are found in or next to fruit orchards, where they feed on the many lizards and small mammals attracted to these areas.

Rainbow and West Indian boas

Variously distributed among the islands of the Caribbean nine species of boa in the genus *Epicrates* originated from perhaps a single ancestor that lived on the South American mainland, where a tenth species, the rainbow boa (*Epicrates cenchria*), survives as a distant relict. At a length of more than 3 m (10 ft), *E. angulifer* from Cuba is much the largest, and three other species, *E. inornatus* (Puerto Rico), *E. subflavus* (Jamaica), and *E. striatus* (Bahamas, Hispaniola), also grow quite large. These snakes are semi-arboreal in habit and feed on a wide variey of prey. Cuban and Puerto Rican boas in particular are known for their habit of catching bats as they emerge at dusk from cave entrances. Among the five smaller species, Haitian vine boas (*E. gracilis*) occur in lowland woods near water, whereas the Mona Island boa (*E. monensis*), is found in dry habitats. Pregnant females of this species are often found in termite nests and may use these sun-baked places for regulating their body temperature.

ABOVE: **The Cuban boa,** *Epicrates angulifer*, **is an inhabitant mostly of forested areas and, although typically found in trees, is equally at home on the ground.**

LEFT: **Rainbow boa,** *Epicrates cenchria*, **an example from Argentina.**

Pacific boas

Three species of boa in the genus *Candoia* are unusual in that they occur in the area of New Guinea and nearby islands, almost as far away from other boas as possible. Their dorsal body scales are strongly keeled, rather than only partially keeled or smooth as they are in most other boas, and they differ also in having a flat, angled rostral scale that gives the snout a distinctly oblique profile. *Candoia aspera* is a small, stout, semi-burrowing inhabitant of the forest floor, *C. carinata* is larger and slimmer, and although mostly terrestrial, is also found in trees, and *C. bibroni*, the largest and most slender is almost exclusively arboreal.

Burrowing boas
Subfamily *Erycinae*

The three genera of boas contained in this subfamily are small, rarely over 1 m (3 ft) long, and largely burrowing in habits. Of the three species of *Charina*, two occur in Pacific North America and one, the rubber boa (*C. bottae*), is found further north than any other boa or python, even ranging into southwestern Canada. This species appears to be especially tolerant of cold; active specimens have been measured with body temperatures of less than 7° C (44° F), although these snakes are unable to withstand the freezing temperatures of

LEFT: **New Guinea viper boa, *Candoia aspera*. The appearance of this small forest floor and semi-aquatic species is similar to the thick-set death adders (*Acanthophis*), and it may be a mimic of these dangerous elapids.**

winter months and at this time hibernate underground.

The rubber boa occurs in many habitats, from dry grasslands to humid woodlands and mountain forests, and may be found at altitudes above 3000 m (9800 ft). North America's other species, the rosy boa (*C. trivirgata*), occurs in drier, desert areas of California and northwestern Mexico. The remaining species, the Calabar boa (*C. reinhardtii*), inhabits forested regions of West Africa. Due to its habit of laying eggs, this unusual snake was long thought to be related to pythons and only recently have biologists found evidence suggesting it has closer affinities with boas. When threatened with danger, rubber and Calabar boas tend to raise the tail to divert attention away from the head, keeping the latter tucked safely beneath their body coils. They may also roll themselves into a tight ball and release a potent musky scent from special anal glands.

ABOVE: **Rough-scaled sand boa, *Gongylophis conicus*.**

BELOW: **The European javelin, or spotted sand boa, *Eryx jaculus*.**

Sand boas

Nine species of sand boas in the genus *Eryx*, and two in *Gongylophis*, are small burrowers that occur over much of Asia and parts of northern Africa. They are particularly suited to life in sandy habitats:

- The skull is compact, and the small conical head has a rounded snout for burrowing in to the sand head-first. In some species the lower jaw is also strongly countersunk, enabling the snakes to feed more easily in narrow burrows.
- The body is cylindrical with a short tail.
- Many species have a hardened, horizontal ridge across the snout.
- The nostrils are on top of the snout, and in many species the openings have been reduced to narrow slits preventing earth and sand being drawn into the respiratory tract.
- Physiological adaptations enable them to reduce water loss and withstand the hot, dry conditions under which many live.

Burrowing boas hunt and feed mostly in underground tunnels, although some sand boas may also ambush prey by hiding in loose sand just beneath the surface, striking upwards at small animals that stumble over them. Rosy boas occasionally forage for food above ground, and rubber boas have even been known to climb trees to raid birds' nests. Most species eat small rodents and lizards, seizing them with a rapid, sidelong, slashing bite. The feeding habits of the rubber and Calabar burrowing boa are particularly unusual. They capture and asphyxiate one or two small mice by trapping them with a coil of the body against the walls of their burrow while simultaneously swallowing another. At the same time they use their short, stubby tail, the terminal vertebrae of which are fused into a bony club, to fend off attacks from the mother mouse. To divert her attention, the snake will even allow her to chew on its tail, so it is perhaps not surprising that the tails of rubber boas found in the wild are almost always heavily scarred!

Pythons
Subfamily *Pythoninae*

African and Asiatic pythons

Of three species of python found in Africa, the most widely distributed and by far the largest is the African rock python (*Python sebae*). These huge snakes occur in dry bush country and forests, and though mostly terrestrial, they climb well and are also semi-aquatic. Among their favourite haunts are river banks, from where they can slip away into the water when danger threatens. The royal python (*P. regius*) of West Africa, and the Angola python (*P. anchietae*) of Angola and the northern half of southwest Africa, are small terrestrial snakes that seldom exceed 2 m (6.5 ft) in length. Named for its handsome and clear-cut markings, the royal python is also called ball python in allusion to its habit of rolling into a tight ball. It occurs mostly in open forests and grasslands, and in parts of its range is quite common, whereas the Angola python is a comparatively rare

RIGHT: **Reticulated python,** ***Python reticulatus.*** **Although primarily terrestrial, this huge python is also an excellent swimmer and was one of the first vertebrates to re-colonize the volcanic island of Krakatau after its catastrophic eruption in 1883.**

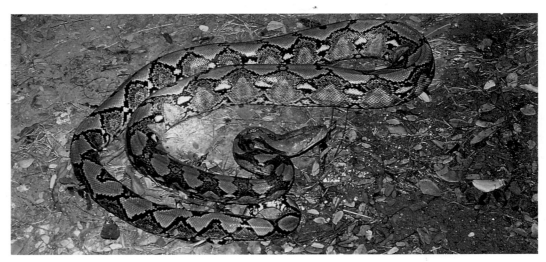

Behavioural secrets of the water python

Owing to their elusive habits and the inherent difficulties of observing them in the wild, the natural lives of many snakes remain to a large extent unknown. One of the few species to have been studied in any great detail is the water python (*Liasis fuscus*), an inhabitant of the seasonally flooded grasslands and billabongs (backwater pools) of northern Australia. By implanting some of these pythons with miniature radio transmitters and monitoring their movements (a process known as radiotelemetry) over several years, Australian biologists have been able to build up a detailed picture of their natural history.

These pythons apparently occupy different habitats and feed on different prey depending on the time of year. During the dry season, they spend the days hidden in dense reedbeds, emerging at dusk to feed more or less exclusively on rats that at this time of year live in the numerous deep cracks of the floodplain mud. Having eaten during the night, the snakes make their way back to the same reeds, where they remain until they need another meal. This pattern of activity continues throughout the dry season until the rains arrive and the rats, having all abandoned their homes to escape the rising water levels, are no longer anywhere to be found. At this time the snakes move out into the spreading floodwaters, where they become more or less completely aquatic and switch to feeding on waterbirds and their eggs. Throughout the wet season they live in these shallow billabongs, concealed among the waterweed and surrounded by literally

ABOVE: **Australian water python, *Liasis fuscus*.**

thousands of plovers, ducks, and other breeding birds.

This ability of water pythons to make use of different resources depending on local conditions is impressive in itself, but an unforeseen event that occurred during the biologists' study inadvertently revealed an even greater flexibility in their behaviour. One of the billabongs that the pythons used as a daytime retreat was emptied for a while to control introduced waterweeds. Deprived of their usual habitat and food supply, the snakes survived by moving away and foraging for prey in the surrounding woodlands, even climbing high into trees, where they remained until the billabong eventually refilled.

BELOW: At 9 m (30 ft) long, the African rock python, *Python sebae*, is exceeded in size perhaps only by the reticulated python. Its diet includes animals up to the size of small antelopes, and there are authentic reports of it also having eaten humans.

species apparently more or less confined to rocky habitats.

Largest of five Asiatic species is the reticulated python (*Python reticulatus*), found in much of equatorial Southeast Asia, including the Philippines and parts of the Indonesian archipelago. Although relatively slender, it is longer than other pythons and may be the world's longest snake (see p. 40). Some individuals may attain lengths well over 9 m (30 ft). It occurs in lowland forests, and although essentially a terrestrial species, it climbs readily and is also often found in water. Another large, mostly terrestrial species is the Asian rock python (*P. molurus*), found over much of the Indian subcontinent and also in parts of Southeast Asia. Like the reticulated python it is an opportunistic ambush predator that may also actively forage for prey. Although much smaller, the short tailed python is distinctive in having a particularly stout, heavy-set body. Usually regarded as a single species with three geographically distinct populations, this

ABOVE: **Sumatran short-tailed python, *Python curtus*. Short-tailed pythons are terrestrial but also spend long periods immersed in muddy swamps or concealed among aquatic vegetation, where they lie in ambush mostly for rodents.**

strikingly marked snake is probably a composite of three separate species, all similar in body proportions and general habits, but varying in scale features and colour patterns. Adult Sumatran short-tailed pythons (*P. curtus*) are dark, almost sooty black, whereas the general body colour of the Borneo species (*P. breitensteini*) is a rich yellow-brown. The mainland species, *P. brongersmai*, is sometimes bright red.

Australian and Indonesian pythons

Many different pythons are widely distributed in Australia, New Guinea, and the many archipelagos associated with this region. Among those from Australia, four species of *Antaresia* are small snakes that rarely exceed 1.5 m (5 ft), and at less than 50 cm (20 in) long, the pygmy python (*A. perthensis*) from the western Pilbara region is the smallest of all pythons. Two other Australian pythons, comprising the genus *Aspidites*, differ from all others in having teeth on the premaxilla, and in lacking supralabial heat-detecting pits. The woma (*A. ramsayi*) occurs in arid habitats throughout much of the continent, while the black-headed python (*A. melanocephalus*)

is known mostly from northern Australia. These snakes eat mostly reptiles, including other snakes.

Largest of the pythons of the Australian–Papuan region is the amethystine python (*Morelia amethystinus*). Widely distributed throughout New Guinea and nearby islands, it also occurs in the Cape York Peninsula of northern Australia. Another Australian 'giant', found only on the dry sandstone escarpments of Arnhem Land in Northern Territory, is the Oenpelli python (*M. oenpelliensis*), famed for having remained undiscovered by scientists until the late 1970s. Adults may attain lengths of over 5 m (16 ft), and can overpower prey up to the size of a small wallaby. From the lowland monsoon forests and flooded savannas of New Guinea, the Papuan python (*Apodora papuana*) is a similarly large species, while Boelen's python (*Morelia boeleni*), also found only in New Guinea, is perhaps the rarest of all pythons. This spectacular-looking snake is black with an overlying purple-blue sheen and a series of bright yellow diagonal streaks. Almost nothing is known of its habits in the wild, other than it occurs in highland forests above 1000 m (3300 ft). Among various other pythons from the Australian–Papuan region, D'Albertis python (*Leiopython albertisii*) is a terrestrial species of lowland rainforests in New Guinea, the green tree python (*Morelia viridis*) is an exclusively arboreal, green snake remarkably similar in appearance to a species of boa in South America (see p. 50), and the Timor python (*Python timorensis*) is a large, semi-arboreal species found only on the islands of Timor and Flores.

Convergent evolution in snakes

Some snakes living in different parts of the world bear a striking resemblance to each other, and but for the often huge distances that separate them, one might easily assume they are closely related. The best known example of this phenomenon is that of the green tree python (*Morelia viridis*), found in Australia and New Guinea, and the emerald tree boa (*Corallus canina*) of South America.

These species are both tree-dwellers that change from yellow or brown as juveniles to bright green as adults. They are the same general size and shape, have similarly shaped heads with greatly enlarged anterior teeth, and also share the same style of resting in trees, looping their bodies over a horizontal branch. Even an expert may have to look twice to work out which is which. The reason why they are so similar, however, is not because they are closely related (both species are grouped in the Boidae but have different ancestral origins), but due to the fact that they live in similar environments and over the course of evolution have been 'moulded' into similar-looking species by the same selective pressures.

ABOVE: **Emerald tree boa,** *Corallus canina.*

LEFT: **Green tree python,** *Morelia viridis.*

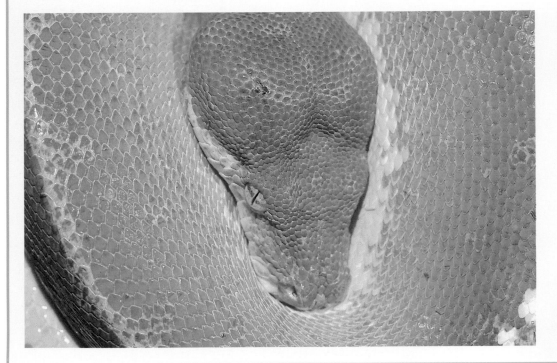

The Round Island Boa

Family *Bolyeriidae*

The boas of Round Island are of particular interest to biologists because of their uncertain origin and isolated distribution. Until recently, two species were known from this small landmass in the Indian Ocean, although owing to large-scale habitat destruction by goats and rabbits introduced in the 19th century, one (*Bolyeria multocarinata*) is probably now extinct. A single individual captured in the mid-1970s was the last to have been seen alive. Subfossil remains of a third, extinct species have been found on the nearby island of Mauritius.

Like the dwarf boas of the family Tropidophiidae, Round Island boas have affinities with the pythons and large boas (Family Boidae), and were long classified as a subfamily of this group. Unlike that of boids, however, the left lung is greatly reduced, and there is no pelvis or vestiges of hind limbs. In respect of these and certain other features they resemble the more evolutionary advanced colubrids. Round Island boas are also unique among snakes in having the maxilla divided into movable front and rear parts.

Bolyeria multocarinata appears to have been a burrowing form, whereas the surviving species, *Casarea dussumieri*, is terrestrial and reaches a length of approximately 1.2 m (4 ft). Nocturnal in habit, it has been found by day hiding beneath fallen palm fronds, in the lower branches of trees, and in burrows excavated by nesting seabirds. It is oviparous, and feeds almost exclusively on the island's few endemic species of geckos and skinks. Although pushed to the brink of extinction, it has responded well to conservation efforts, and its numbers on the island have now started to recover.

Dwarf Boas
Family *Tropidophiidae*

In certain features of anatomy, the four genera of small boa-like forms in this family resemble the large, more distinguished boas of the family Boidae, and may have arisen from an early branch of the latter group in South America. With two exceptions (*Tropidophis semicinctus* and female *Ungaliophis*) they share the primitive feature of a pectoral girdle and, in males of most species, external vestiges of hind limbs. Unlike the large boas and their relatives, however, tropidophiids have a well-developed tracheal lung, and the left lung is greatly reduced or lacking altogether. The snakes of this family also have affinities with the geographically distant Round Island boas (Bolyeriidae).

Dwarf boas are small snakes, with bodies that are cylindrical or flattened from side to side, and most have relatively short, prehensile tails. They are secretive and essentially nocturnal inhabitants of the forest floor, although the two species of *Ungaliophis* and several *Tropidophis* are at least partially arboreal. Most are active foragers, feeding mainly on lizards and frogs, which they kill by constriction. The larger species of *Tropidophis* may occasionally also feed on small rodents and nestling birds. Except for *Trachyboa gularis*, all species are viviparous.

Dwarf boas occur in Central America, northern South America, and the Caribbean islands, and are divided into two subfamilies according to the structure of their hemipenes.

'Wood snakes' and eyelash dwarf boas
Subfamily *Tropidophiinae*

Prominent among the snakes of this subfamily are 17 species of *Tropidophis*, most of which are distributed among the islands of the Caribbean, where the scarcity of other snakes and perhaps other favourable circumstances has permitted these otherwise primitive forms to diversify and exploit a wide range of habitats. The genus is best represented on Cuba, with 11 species. Three species survive as relicts on the South American mainland, ranging from Ecuador (*T. battersbyi*) to Peru and Brazil (*T. paucisquamis* and *T. taczanowskyi*).

Most *Tropidophis* are dull brown or grey snakes with a variable pattern of dorsal body blotches and spots. Three Cuban species, *T. semicinctus*, *T. spiritus*, and *T. wrightii*, are more conspicuously marked than most, with patterns of light and dark bands or blotches. The scales on the dorsum are keeled in some species and smooth in others. Commonly called 'wood snakes', *Tropidophis* occur predominantly in forested habitats, ranging from humid rainforest to dry *Acacia*-cactus scrub; a recently described Cuban species, *T. fuscus*, is known only from pine woods associated with red lateritic soils in the eastern part of the island. Most *Tropidophis* are terrestrial and typically found beneath

ABOVE: **At slightly over 1 m (3.3 ft) long,** *Tropidophis melanurus*, **from Cuba, is among the largest of the 'wood snakes'. This orange-coloured example is one of two main colour forms.**

logs, fallen palm fronds and other forest floor debris, and in ant and termite nests.

Avoiding predators

Tropidophis are unique among snakes for their extraordinary ability to autohaemorrhage, a curious form of behaviour which appears to have evolved as a defence reaction. If attacked, their eyes turn red with blood, and the mouth begins to bleed freely from veins on the palate. Although alarming to observe, this does not seem to have any detrimental effect on the snake and, when danger has

passed, it will quickly recover. If molested, a *Tropidophis* may also coil up in a small ball with its head hidden in the centre, and produce an offensive-smelling anal secretion.

Various other snakes (all North American colubrids) are reputed to adopt 'bleeding' behaviour. Long-nosed snakes (*Rhinocheilus lecontei*) and eastern hognosed snakes (*Heterodon platyrhinos*) bleed from the cloaca, while the yellow-bellied water snake (*Nerodia erythrogaster*) sometimes exudes blood from the gums. In these species the bleeding may be incidental, caused by the wild thrashing they often resort to when molested, but in *Tropidophis* it appears to be more controlled.

Forest-floor inhabitants

The remaining genus of the Tropidophiinae, *Trachyboa*, contains two small, stout-bodied snakes with an extremely short tail and strongly keeled scales. *T. boulengeri* has one or more enlarged, projecting scales over the eye and similar horn-like scales on the canthus (contour of the snout between the top and side of the head), a feature that has given rise to the name 'eyelash dwarf boa', by which both species are known. They feed almost exclusively on small frogs.

T. boulengeri occurs in the humid lowland rainforests of Costa Rica, Panama, Ecuador, and Colombia, while the other species, *T. gularis*, is found in the dry coastal forests of western Ecuador.

'Banana boas' and the Oaxacan dwarf boa
Subfamily *Ungaliophiinae*

There are two genera in this subfamily: *Ungaliophis* contains two species with separate distributions in Central America, and *Exiliboa placata* is restricted to high-altitude cloud forests of Oaxaca, Mexico. The configuration of the head scales in these species is particularly distinctive. In *Ungaliophis*, the prefrontals are coalesced and expanded over much of the snout, whereas in *Exiliboa*, which has the more usual condition

OPPOSITE: **Banana boa,** *Ungaliophis panamensis.*

BELOW: **Eyelash dwarf ground boa,** *Trachyboa boulengeri*. **These distinctive-looking, slow-moving snakes forage on the surface, where their roughened scales and muted brown colour conceals them among leaves and other forest-floor debris.**

of paired prefrontals, it is the internasals that are fused, forming a single, large, triangular-shaped plate.

Occasional specimens of Ungaliophis reaching the USA in shipments of bananas have led to them becoming popularly known as 'banana boas'. Their maxillary teeth are somewhat more specialized than in other dwarf boas, and are perhaps modified for feeding on small, tree-dwelling frogs and lizards, their chief prey. The northern species, *U. continentalis*, lives mainly at low to intermediate altitudes from Chiapas, southern Mexico, to Honduras, though it is also known from above 2000 m (6600 ft) in the

Colour change in snakes

Several species of *Tropidophis*, and some other snakes, too, have the unusual ability to change colour, a curious phenomenon that appears to be associated with activity and generally follows a 24-hour cycle. Perhaps the most striking is that demonstrated in *T. haetianus* which, when active at night, has a pale yellow ground colour with two rows of dark dorsal markings, but during the day is almost completely black. *T. feicki* undergoes similar daily colour changes and should this species be subjected to a temperature of less than 17°C (63°F), it will adopt a transitional colour phase at any time of the day.

Colour change has also been reported in various other snakes, including *Boa constrictor*, Pacific boas (*Candoia bibroni* and *C. carinata*), the Round Island boa (*Casarea dussumieri*), the western rattlesnake (*Crotalus viridis*) and most notably, the giant Oenpelli python (*Morelia oenpelliensis*) of northern Australia, which changes from a drab brown during the day to a ghostly silver-grey at night. Darkening occurs when melanophores (pigment-containing cell structures) in the epidermis (outermost skin layer) are moved closer to the skin's surface, and is probably controlled by hormonal cues. Colour change in snakes may also be developmental in origin. Mussuranas (*Clelia clelia*) from Central and South America, for example, are bright red with a black head and pale neck collar as juveniles, whereas at about 0.6 m (2 ft) in length they change quite abruptly to uniform black or dark bluish-grey. Similarly, some arboreal, green species undergo a striking colour change with age. Young green tree pythons (*Morelia viridis*), from New Guinea and Australia, and emerald tree boas (*Corallus canina*), from South America, for example, are yellow or orange-brown at first, while juvenile green cat snakes, *Boiga cyanea*, from Southeast Asia, are mainly brownish. Researchers do not fully understand why adults and juveniles of these particular snakes are so differently coloured.

Some snakes also undergo seasonal changes in colour, usually in response to reproductive cues. After they emerge from hibernation in spring, for example, the general ground colour of male European adders (*Vipera berus*) is a resplendent silver-grey, whereas after the reproductive season has finished they become drabber.

LEFT: **Restricted to high elevation cloud forests in Central Mexico, the Oaxacan dwarf boa, *Exiliboa placata*, is a little known species that feeds on frogs. It immobilizes prey by constriction.**

pine forests of eastern Chiapas. *Ungaliophis panamensis*, the southern species, is found from southeastern Nicaragua through Costa Rica and Panama into northern Colombia. Adult *Ungaliophis* attain an overall length of about 70 cm (2.3 ft). They are nocturnal and mainly arboreal.

Isolated distribution

The remaining species of this group, the Oaxacan dwarf boa (*Exiliboa palacata*) is found only in the cool, moist forests that prevail at 2000–3000 m (6600–9800 ft) on the mountain slopes of Oaxaca, Mexico. No other dwarf boas occur in this region, and neither are many other species of reptile found here. The generic name *Exiliboa* comes from the Latin 'exigere', 'to banish', in allusion to its isolated occurrence. A small snake, perhaps reaching no more than 50 cm (20 in), its body is compressed towards the base of the tail, where it is appreciably higher than wide, and external vestiges of limbs are present in both sexes. The dorsum is almost uniformly black, the only conspicuous mark being a white patch that covers the anal scute. Specialized for burrowing in wet leaf litter, it preys mainly on small frogs.

File Snakes
Family *Acrochordidae*

The file snakes, or 'wart snakes', are so called because of the coarse, granular appearance of their scales. They form a distinctive family consisting of one genus (*Acrochordus*), with three species. In size and body proportions these unusual snakes resemble some pythons and boas, although in other features, such as a single functional lung, absence of a pelvis and hind limbs, and certain features of the skull and jaw bones, they appear to be more closely related to the 'typical' colubrid snakes.

Aquatic specialists

File snakes are entirely aquatic. They occur mostly in estuarine and freshwater habitats, although the little file snake (*Acrochordus granulatus*) may also be found in coastal marine waters, often in areas frequented by true sea snakes. Much like sea snakes, file snakes have acquired a series of external and internal modifications that enable them to take full advantage of their aquatic surroundings (see p. 95).

The most conspicuous feature of these snakes is their skin, which is loose and baggy, and covered with small, tubercular (wart-like), non-overlapping scales. There are no broad, transverse scales on the abdomen, and the scales on the head are also all of the same general shape and form. Few other large snakes have such small, evenly-sized scales on both the dorsal and ventral surfaces of the body, and this particular quality has made the

ABOVE: **Javan file snake,** *Acrochordus javanicus*. **File snakes range in distribution from India through much of Indo-China and Southeast Asia to the South Pacific region and northern Australia.**

Male or female?

There are few distinguishing features between male and female snakes. Sexual dimorphism in these animals is typically limited externally to subtle differences in tail length, and the relative numbers of scales on the abdomen (ventrals) and underside of the tail (subcaudals), although there are a number that differ more noticeably. Madagascan leaf-nosed snakes (*Langaha nasuta*), for example have differently shaped appendages on the snout, while males and females of some sea snakes have different colour patterns.

Perhaps the most sexually dimorphic snake studied to date, however, is the Arafura file snake (*Acrochordus arafurae*). Females of this species are conspicuously larger and more heavy-bodied than males, have relatively larger heads and jaws, and shorter tails. An adult female may attain a length of 2 m (6.6 ft) and weigh more than 2 kg (4.4 lb), whereas the much smaller male rarely exceeds 1 m (3.3 ft) in length and averages considerably less than 1 kg (2.2 lb) in weight. Even when males and females are about the same length, the female's head is proportionally larger and its body much more heavy-set. These differences are apparent even in newborns.

Divergence in body size between the sexes of Arafura file snakes has probably arisen through evolutionary selection for reproductive success – the larger the female's body, the larger her capacity for producing more offspring in a litter. The difference in relative head and jaw sizes, however, appears to be more the result of adaptations of males and females to different ecological niches rather than sexual selection – the sexes have undergone independent specialization over time to take advantage of different food resources and thereby increase their success rates in hunting. Females have been shown to hunt in deeper water than males and generally eat only a single large fish, whereas males tend to inhabit shallower water and eat a larger number of smaller fish. As adults, the sexes also feed on different species of fish.

skin of *Acrochordus* highly prized in the leather trade. In Southeast Asia, many thousand *A. granulatus* are harvested for this purpose every year, the tanned skins of which are sold as 'Karung' (see p. 10).

File snakes feed exclusively on fish. They may seize prey with a sudden sideways snap, although they more typically entrap it within their body loops and subdue it by constriction. The coarse, 'gritty' nature of the scales helps restrain the slippery, struggling prey and prevent it from escaping. Observations of wild, free-ranging *Acrochordus arafurae* show that these snakes have very low feeding rates and may eat prey only a few times each year. File snakes are viviparous and female *A. arafurae* in particular produce large numbers of offspring, although this species reproduces less frequently than do most other snakes, perhaps as little as once every 10 years.

Low metabolism

File snakes have an unusually low rate of metabolism, only about half that of other snakes, and appear incapable of sustained activity for more than a few minutes. Out of the water they are sluggish and seem almost helpless. Studies of *Acrochordus arafurae*, however, have shown that these snakes, although slow in their movements, are suprisingly active and capable of travelling for considerable distances in the seasonally flooded billabongs of northern Australia where they occur. During the day they remain hidden under overhanging banks, beneath sunken logs, or amongst waterweed, but while searching for food at night they frequently cover distances of several hundred metres.

Burrowing Asps
Family *Atractaspididae*

These essentially venomous snakes represent a somewhat unconventional group in that they include species with different dentition and biting mechanisms. Most have fixed, grooved fangs in the rear of the mouth, in which respect they resemble the rear-fanged (opisthoglyphous) colubrids, while others have hollow, movable, front-mounted fangs like those of vipers. Atractaspids, or burrowing asps, as they may be collectively called, mostly live underground and are highly adapted for burrowing. Their bodies are cylindrical and of about the same circumference throughout, with no discernible narrowing at the neck. The skull is compact, and the small head often has a projecting snout. Many species have tiny eyes. The tail is typically very short, and in some species bears a sharp spine at its tip. Some of the larger species grow to just over 1 m (3.3 ft), though most are considerably smaller.

Several atractaspids are sufficiently dangerous to be considered medically important. The bite of the Natal black snake (*Macrelaps microlepidotus*), in particular, has been known to result in a temporary loss of consciousness, and bites from the larger species of *Atractaspis* may also have serious consequences. The venom is predominantly neurotoxic in its effect (see p. 17–19), although it also produces local swelling, severe pain, and other symptoms more typical of viper bites.

The Atractaspididae is essentially African in distribution, with some species ranging into the Near East, and occurs in habitats as diverse as rainforest, grasslands, and semi-desert. Except for one species, Jackson's centipede-eater (*Aparallactus jacksonii*), they are all viviparous.

Stiletto snakes
Subfamily *Atractaspidinae*

A group of 18 species contained within a single genus, *Atractaspis*, the stiletto snakes, or 'mole vipers', are remarkable for their disproportionately large, hollow fangs, which are erected independently of each other and extended downwards into a biting position without opening the jaws. There are typically two fangs on each side, one functional and the other a replacement. All other maxillary teeth have been lost, and except for a few on the palatine bones and two or three on the dentaries, the mouth has no other teeth. The venom-injecting apparatus of *Atractaspis*

BELOW: **Skull of stiletto snake. Note the enormous fangs. On the basis of their dentition, *Atractaspis* species were long believed to be vipers. Unlike vipers, however, the fang-bearing maxillary bone pivots on a lateral ball and socket joint, and the fangs cannot be rotated forwards.**

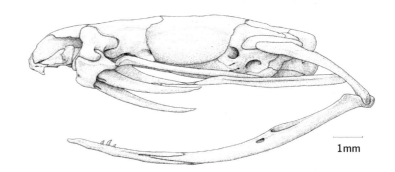

1mm

ABOVE: **Duerden's stiletto snake, *Atractraspis duerdeni*.** Stiletto snakes are found throughout much of Africa, with some species ranging into the drier northern part of the continent and also across large areas of Arabia and Israel.

is unusual in a number of other respects, too. Each fang bears a small cutting edge opposite its orifice, and the venom gland in some species, such as the small-scaled stiletto snake (*A. microlepidota*), is extraordinarily long, extending under the skin behind the head for approximately 15% of the body length. The venom itself also has a special composition (see p. 18).

Feeding and predator evasion

Stiletto snakes hunt and feed underground, largely on rodents and their nestlings, and, without the need to open the mouth to bite, are capable of killing prey in the most restricted of spaces. In delivering the predatory strike, a single fang is erected from whichever side of the head is next to the animal, and jerked sideways, downwards, and backwards with a quick 'stabbing' movement.

The rotating maxilla displaces the upper lip, thus opening a slit through which the fang can be extended. Should a foraging snake encounter more than one rodent at a time, it will typically bite and immobilize all available prey before beginning to feed, and may consume the occupants of an entire nest of mice in this manner if presented with the opportunity. Skinks, amphisbaenians (worm-lizards), frogs, and other snakes are also eaten.

In response to an assault from a predator, stiletto snakes will arch the neck and strike rapidly with a slashing backwards movement. They bite with little provocation, and owing to their peculiar fang erection mechanism and the unusual flexibility of the neck vertebrae, are almost impossible to restrain safely if handled. If molested, an *Atractaspis* may also use the tail-distraction ruse (see p. 26).

Centipede-eaters and their allies
Subfamily *Aparallactinae*

Aparallactine snakes typically have one or two enlarged, grooved fangs that are situated towards the rear of the mouth and preceded, but not followed, by three to ten smaller, ungrooved teeth. Unlike those of stiletto snakes, the fangs are non-erectile. One species of centipede-eater, *Aparallactus modestus*, and the snakes of the genus *Poecilophotis* differ in having uniformly-sized, ungrooved maxillary teeth, and *Poecilopholis* species also lack a venom-secreting (Duvernoy's) gland.

Species diversity in the Aparallactinae

The monotypic Natal blacksnake (*Macrelaps microlepidotus*), an inhabitant of damp places near water, has the least specialized diet, eating rodents, frogs, legless lizards, and a variety of other small vertebrates. Many of the remaining nine genera, however, have markedly diverse feeding habits.

The 11 species of *Aparallactus* have one of the most unusual dietary habits of any snake. They feed almost exclusively on centipedes, and have enlarged anterior mandibular teeth that perhaps enable them to grasp more effectively the hard, chitinous exoskeletons of these formidable invertebrates. Once bitten, a violent struggle often ensues until the envenomated centipede, which may be over 12 cm (5 in) long and nearly twice the diameter of the snake's body, is sufficiently disabled for the snake to swallow it. The bite of the centipede, which is itself venomous, appears to have little effect on these snakes. *Aparallactus* occur in rainforest, open bush, sandy regions, and savanna, where they are found among roots, beneath stones or fallen logs, and in termite mounds. In general appearance many resemble snakes of the New World colubrid genera *Tantilla* and *Tantillita*, which are also rear-fanged and feed on centipedes.

Nine species of purple-glossed snakes (*Amblyodipsas*) – the common name refers to the purplish sheen of their dark-coloured bodies – are rather stout-bodied snakes in which females appear to grow larger than males. At an adult length of 1 m (3.3 ft), female common purple-glossed snakes (*A. polylepsis*) are almost twice as large as their mates. These species feed largely on reptiles, including limbless lizards, blind snakes, and amphisbaenians.

BELOW: **Centipede-eater,** *Aparallactus capensis*.

ABOVE: **Quill-snouted snake, *Xenocalamus bicolor*.**

A group of five unusual-looking quill-snouted snakes (*Xenocalamus*) derive their name from the resemblance of the prominently undercut mouth to that of a quill pen. These species have exceptionally slender and elongate bodies, with flattened heads, minute eyes, and acutely pointed snouts with a conspicuously enlarged rostral scale. They occur mostly in sandy regions and feed exclusively on amphisbaenians, often selecting single prey species at a particular locality. Attractively marked with alternating stripes of yellow and black, three species of *Chilorhinophis* are semi-burrowing forms that also live largely on a diet of amphisbaenians. The tails of these snakes are coloured and shaped much like the head, and used in distracting predators (see p. 26).

Rat Snakes, Racers, Garter Snakes and Relatives

Family *Colubridae*

Largest of all snake families, the Colubridae comprises some 300 genera and perhaps more than 1500 species, over half the world's snakes. Colubrids are found on all continents except Antarctica and form the main element of snake faunas almost everywhere; only in Australia, where the elapids predominate, are they in the minority. All species lack a pelvic girdle, a functional left lung, and the coronoid bone (a small bone in the lower jaw retained by primitive snakes). Some are aglyphous, with unmodified teeth, while others are opisthoglyphous, with enlarged, grooved maxillary fangs towards the back of the upper jaw (see p. 8), usually connected to a poison-producing salivary gland (Duvernoy's gland). Usually, the venom of these species is lethal only to the animals they feed upon, though there are a few whose bites are dangerous and have resulted in human deaths (see p. 78–79).

In size, they range from diminutive centipede-eating snakes (genera *Tantilla* and *Tantillita*) little longer than a pencil, to the 3.8 m (12.5 ft) long Asian keeled rat snake (*Ptyas carinatus*), and while many are generalist predators that feed on a wide variety of different prey, others have special adaptations for highly restricted diets. So great is the range of different characters exhibited by colubrid snakes that herpetologists are forever trying to reshuffle them into more meaningful groups. Most recognize ten or more subfamilies, but it is likely that they will split some into smaller groups and promote others to full family status. In the absence of any generally agreed scheme of classification, the snakes of this family are discussed here under groupings that, while reflecting to some extent current scientific opinion, do not place too much emphasis on classification. With so many different species we can sample only a very small number of them in this concise account. In making this selection, however, we feature as broad a cross-section of species as possible, and include examples of particular interest.

BELOW: **While most colubrids are egg-layers, the European smooth snake (*Coronella austriaca*) is among a small number of species that give birth to live young.**

ABOVE: **Tiger rat snake,** *Spilotes pullatus*. **Although primarily an inhabitant of forests, this large species from tropical America also thrives around farms and rural settlements, where it feeds on vermin, and domestic fowl and their eggs.**

OPPOSITE: **The slender body and large eyes with round pupils of this Central American racer,** *Dryadophis melanolomus*, **are characteristic of a fast-moving, diurnal species that hunts down prey by sight, in this case lizards.**

Rat snakes, king snakes, racers, tree snakes and egg-eaters

More often referred to as typical snakes, rat snakes, racers, and king snakes are among a diverse mixture of genera usually included within the subfamily Colubrinae. At least some have almost certainly evolved independently and at some point are likely to be reclassified.

Rat snakes, king snakes and allies

Among the largest are two species of Asian rat snakes, *Ptyas carinatus* and *P. mucosus*, both of which are reported to exceed lengths of 3.5 m (11.5 ft), and there are others that also grow to considerable sizes. The indigo snake (*Drymarchon corais*), in particular, may occasionally exceed 3 m (10 ft) and is almost as robust as some boas and pythons. This widespread New World species occurs in a number of different geographic forms throughout much of Central and South America, extending northwards into southern USA. It is a generalist predator that eats a wide variety of vertebrate prey, especially other snakes, and it has a voracious appetite. A 2.95 m (9.7 ft) long example from Guatemala caught in the act of swallowing a 1.6 m (5.2 ft) long common boa (*Boa constrictor*) already had in its stomach a

65

typically active snakes that hunt by day. Many have conspicuously large eyes and those of eight tropical American species in the genus *Dendrophidion* are especially prominent. They feed chiefly on lizards and frogs, but larger species will also eat small mammals, birds, and other snakes. Although primarily terrestrial, they may be found high above the ground in trees, and some are adept at climbing.

Tree Snakes

Among many colubrines that have enlarged fangs in the rear of the mouth and immobilize prey by injecting venom, two in particular are capable of inflicting lethally dangerous bites (see p. 78–79). Vine snakes (*Oxybelis* from tropical America and *Ahaetulla* from Asia), include day-active species that spend almost all their lives in the trees and descend to the ground only rarely. They typically have long, exceptionally slender bodies and narrow pointed heads with large eyes, and most species have relatively keen eyesight. Other rear-fanged, day-active, tree-living colubrines include five species of Asian flying snakes (*Chrysopelea*), which escape from predators in the treetops by launching themselves off a branch and descending down to the ground or a lower branch in a long, controlled glide.

full- grown jumping pit viper (*Atropoides nummifer*), itself almost 1 m (3.3 ft) in length.

A group of colubrines that constrict their prey and occur mostly in temperate regions include eight species of king snakes (*Lampropeltis*) and five species of gopher snakes (*Pituophis*) from the Americas, and various rat snakes (e.g. *Bogertophis*, *Elaphe*, *Senticolis*). Many of these feed on rodents, although their diets typically include a wide range of other prey. King snakes will often eat other snakes, and common king snakes (*L. getulus*) will not hesitate to attack rattlesnakes, copperheads, coral snakes, and other dangerously venomous species.

Racers

Noted for their agility and speed of movement are various genera of slender-bodied snakes collectively known as 'racers'. About 40 species in the genus *Coluber* include a widespread and often locally abundant species in North America (*C. constrictor*), and others in Europe and Asia. Racers are

ABOVE: **From Mediterranean Europe, the leopard snake, *Elaphe situla*, is a colourful rat snake of olive groves, woods, and rocky hillsides. It feeds on lizards and small mammals.**

BELOW: **The coachwhip, *Masticophis flagellum*, from North America is a large racer-like species that occasionally exceeds lengths of 2.5 m (8 ft).**

Sometimes grouped in a separate tribe or subfamily, the Boiginae, several genera of nocturnal rear-fanged colubrines include 28 species of Old World cat snakes (genus *Boiga*) that have slender bodies, flattened from side to side, and large eyes with vertically-elliptic pupils. Essentially tree-dwellers, some grow to impressive sizes. The dog-toothed cat snake (*B. cynodon*) from Southeast Asia, and Indonesia in particular, may occasionally attain lengths over 2.75 m (9 ft). A strikingly marked black-and-yellow banded species from Southeast Asia, the mangrove snake (*B. dendrophila*) is relatively stout-bodied and also has a broader diet than most of its relatives, feeding on bats, birds and their eggs, lizards, frogs, other snakes, and even fish. Bites from some species can lead to severe poisoning. Other nocturnal rear-fanged cat snakes include more than a dozen species of

ABOVE: **Green cat snake, *Boiga cyanea*, a rear-fanged arboreal species from Southeast Asia.**

BELOW: **Asian vine snakes (genus *Ahaetulla*) have unusual keyhole-shaped pupils, binocular vision, and a long grooved snout, which gives them a wide field of view. This species is *A. nasuta* from India and parts of Southeast Asia.**

Telescopus, among which African tiger snakes (*T. beetzii* and *T. semiannulatus*) are strikingly marked yellow- and black-spotted snakes that feed mostly on geckos and other lizards, but will sometimes climb into trees to rob birds' nests of their eggs and nestlings.

African marsh snakes, keelbacks, garter snakes and water snakes

These well-known snakes are among several genera of mostly semi-aquatic species traditionally grouped in the subfamily Natricinae. They are widespread in the Old World, and there are many species also in North America, including Canada, Mexico and Central America. Most Old World species lay eggs, whereas the American forms are viviparous.

Egg-eating snakes

Various colubrids have highly specialized feeding habits. Conspicuous among these are six species of African egg-eating snakes (genus *Dasypeltis*), which feed exclusively on birds' eggs and have special structures for dealing with their smooth, hard shells. On the underside of the neck vertebrae are a series of 25–35 bony spines (the hypapophyses) that project downwards like teeth and actually penetrate through into the gullet. As the snake swallows an egg, it performs a series of sideways and downward rocking movements with its head, during which the egg is rubbed against these vertebral 'teeth' until ultimately it breaks, often with an audible cracking sound; muscular contractions of the oesophagus then compress the shell and release its contents into the stomach. The snake expels the crushed empty shell shortly afterwards through its mouth.

So remarkably extensible is the mouth of an egg-eating snake that even comparatively large eggs can be swallowed whole. A 1 m (3.3 ft) long snake with a head scarcely wider than a large finger nail, for example, is quite capable of consuming an average sized chicken's egg. Such incredible feats of swallowing are made possible by a number of modifications that primarily affect the skull. In particular, the supratemporal bones and quadrates (see p. 9) are greatly elongated; in most snakes these bones are movably jointed, but in egg-eaters they are fused into an especially movable, free-swinging structure. Furthermore, the lower jaw is rather long and the ligament that connects each side at the front is highly elastic, enabling the two halves to be stretched widely apart. Inside the mouth itself, there are also loose folds of skin that lie along the lower jaw and unravel during swallowing.

Among various other snakes that eat eggs, the Japanese rat snake (*Elpahe climacophora*) also has spines on the underside of a few anterior vertebrae, but this and all other species swallow them whole and digest everything, including the shell. Only the African egg-eating snakes and maybe a poorly known Indian species, *Elachistodon westermanni*, crush and regurgitate the shells.

LEFT: **Egg-eating snake, *Dasypeltis scabra.***

Marsh snakes

Natricines from tropical Africa include three species of marsh snakes (genus *Natriciteres*) and various other water-dwelling species (*Afronatrix* and *Hydraethiops*) that feed chiefly on frogs. Some also eat fish and aquatic invertebrates. Marsh snakes are unusual in being able to break off their tails to escape from predators, although unlike that of many lizards, the tail does not grow back once broken. Among the most widespread, the African olive marsh snake (*N. olivacea*) ranges from Ghana and Sudan to Angola, Zimbabwe, and southern Mozambique, in streams and marshes from sea level up to about 1980 m (6500 ft).

Keelbacks

Asian natricines include various genera, collectively called 'keelbacks', that live in a wide range of habitats and feed mainly on amphibians and fish. Among the most widespread, ten species of *Xenochrophis* are largely aquatic. The chequered keelback (*X. piscator*) is a particularly common species found throughout much of southern Asia where it occurs in weed-choked ponds, slow-flowing rivers, streams, ditches, and flooded rice paddies. Notable among Asian keelbacks for their potentially dangerous bites are 18 species in the genus *Rhabdophis*. Most are generally mild-mannered and docile, but they have much-enlarged rear fangs and the venom of at least two species is unusually toxic (see p. 79). Many Asian natricines flatten their necks when alarmed, and *Macropisthodon* and some species of *Rhabdophis* discharge a distasteful whitish

From much of Europe, northwest Africa and Asia, 6 species in the genus *Natrix* are day-active snakes that feed mainly on frogs, newts, tadpoles, and small fish. They are usually found in or near water, although some are more aquatic than others. The dice snake (*N. tessellata*) in particular, spends much of its time in water and often remains beneath the surface for considerable periods, while others may often be encountered in dry heathlands, meadows and woods. European *Natrix* are mostly green snakes marked with variable patterns of spots or indistinct stripes, although the viperine snake (*N. maura*) often has a zigzag pattern that increases its resemblance to a viper. By hissing fiercely, flattening its body, and striking repeatedly (though usually with its mouth closed) when cornered, the behaviour of this species is also convincingly viper-like.

ABOVE: **Grass snake, *Natrix natrix*, a particularly wide-ranging European species that occurs as far north as 67°N in Scandinavia, and in the southern Alps reaches altitudes up to 2400 m (7900 ft).**

A plundering vagrant – the brown cat snake on Guam

In the 1960s biologists on the small Pacific island of Guam began to notice that its native bird populations were beginning to decline markedly. This trend continued through the 1970s and 1980s until, by 1987, all ten species of birds that inhabited the island's forests appeared to be in serious trouble; two found only on Guam and nowhere else, the Guam flycatcher (*Myiagra freycineti*) and the Guam rail (*Gallirallus owstoni*), had not been seen for several years, and a previously widespread seabird, the white tern (*Gygis alba*), had become mysteriously restricted to the northern coastline. Native bats and lizards had also declined drastically. A variety of possible causes for this were investigated, including disease, parasites, and habitat alteration, but it ultimately became clear that the catastrophe was attributable to a snake,

the brown cat snake (*Boiga irregularis*). Indigenous to northeastern Australia, New Guinea, and adjacent islands, this 3 m (10 ft) long rear-fanged venomous species had been accidentally introduced to Guam on cargo shipments shortly after World War II, and by 1982 was common almost everywhere on the island, except in a few small areas of savanna.

That a snake could be capable of establishing itself in such numbers as to almost decimate the bird population of an entire island was at first difficult for many to comprehend. Snakes are efficient predators but do not normally occur in large numbers anywhere (although interestingly one of the few species that does also lives on an island and feeds exclusively on birds: see p. 106). Experiments using traps suspended in trees and baited with quails, however, showed beyond doubt that the brown cat snake was

indeed the culprit; in areas where native birds had disappeared, 75% of traps had been sprung and the quails devoured within just a few days. It was not only the local wildlife on Guam that suffered. Brown cat snakes have a potent neurotoxic venom and several young children bitten by them while sleeping suffered serious symptoms. By raiding chicken farms and causing many power failures by climbing into transformers and onto overhead cables, the snakes also levied a heavy toll on the island's economy.

In an effort to restore the island in some way to its former natural ecological balance, the numbers of brown cat snakes on Guam are gradually being reduced by trapping, and several zoos are also maintaining populations of the surviving bird species with a view to re-establishing them in the wild. For some of its birds, however, remedial action on Guam has arrived too late.

RIGHT: **Brown cat snake,** *Boiga irregularis*.

secretion at the same time from glands in the neck. A group of 16 species found mostly in highland areas, the stream snakes (genus *Opisthotropis*) eat mostly earthworms, while the bicoloured stream snake (*O. lateralis*) resembles some North American swamp snakes (genus *Regina*) in its striped body markings and diet of crustaceans.

Garter snakes

Among the most widespread and common natricines in North America are the 26 species of garter and ribbon snakes (genus *Thamnophis*). Several range into southern Canada and some also live in Mexico and northern Central America. Often brightly coloured, with contrasting patterns of dorsal stripes and spots, they are small to medium-sized, rather slender snakes with strongly keeled scales. Northwestern garter snakes

ABOVE: **Green water snake, *Nerodia cyclopion*, largest of the North American water snakes and one of the most fecund snakes in this region; adult females may produce more than 100 young in a single litter.**

LEFT: **Garter snakes are found in a wide range of different habitats but usually near pools and other bodies of freshwater. Among the more thoroughly aquatic is the twin-striped garter snake, *Thamnophis hammondi*, from southern California and Mexico.**

(*T. ordinoides*) and Western terrestrial garter snakes (*T. elegans*), in particular, are often found far from water, while others, such as Western aquatic garter snakes (*T. couchi*) and narrow-headed garter snakes (*T. rufopunctatus*) are highly aquatic. Garter and ribbon snakes feed chiefly on amphibians, small fish, earthworms, and aquatic invertebrates such as leeches.

Water snakes

Widely distributed over large parts of eastern and southern North America are 12 species of highly aquatic water snakes (*Nerodia*). These are stout-bodied forms with strongly keeled dorsal scales and sombre-colored markings. Females often grow considerably larger than males and those of some species, such as the green water snakes (*N. cyclopion* and *N. floridana*) and the brown water snake (*N. taxispilota*), may occasionally grow to over 1.5 m (5 ft). Water snakes are almost always found near ponds, streams, bayous, canals and lakes, particularly where there is dense aquatic vegetation and little current, although Harter's water snake (*N. harteri*) of Texas is restricted mostly to clear, swift-flowing streams and rivers, and salt-marsh snakes (*N. clarkii*) occur mostly in brackish estuaries.

Other water-living natricines from North America include the black swamp snake (*Seminatrix pygaea*) and four species of crayfish snakes (*Regina*). These thoroughly aquatic species are typically found coiled among the matted roots of water hyacinth and other floating vegetation, where they feed on frogs, small fish, shrimp, crayfish, and other aquatic invertebrates. Crayfish, in particular, feature heavily in the diets of several species, and the queen snake (*Regina septemvittata*) appears to feed almost exclusively on newly-moulted crayfish whose shells have not yet hardened. The four species of brown and red-

BELOW: **Bull snake, *Pituophis catenifer*, a large and powerfully-built constrictor from North America noted for its rodent-eating habits and aggressive nature.**

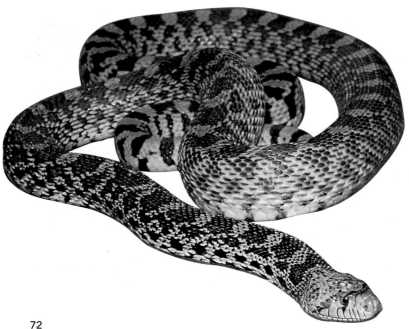

bellied snakes (genus *Storeria*), three of earth snakes (*Virginia*), and Kirtland's snake (*Clonophis kirtlandi*) are among a number of other North American and Mexican natricines that, although often found near water, are entirely terrestrial. These species mostly eat invertebrates and live among leaf litter in wooded areas or grass in wet meadows.

Tentacled snakes, mangrove snakes and other Old World aquatics

Ten genera and approximately 32 species in the subfamily Homalopsinae are highly aquatic water snakes from Southeast Asia and coastal northern Australia. They are found in both freshwater and marine environments, and have various specializations for aquatic life, such as nostrils set on the end of the snout that can be closed by valves when submerging, and small upwardly-facing eyes. All species are rear-fanged and some bite fiercely when handled, although they are not regarded as dangerously toxic to humans. Most are smallish snakes with relatively thick-set bodies, the longest and stoutest being Bocourt's water snake, *Enhydris bocourti*, about 1 m (3.3 ft) long, from West Malaysia, Cambodia, Thailand, and Vietnam. Another Southeast Asian species of river mouths and coastal waters, the keel-bellied water snake (*Bitia hydroides*) has features more typically associated with some sea snakes, such as a small head and neck tapering to a proportionally large body, reduced ventral scales, and a tail flattened from side to side.

Homalopsines feed mostly on fish, which they capture by ambush or by feeling around for them in muddy water. The tentacled snake (*Erpeton tantaculatus*) has long, paired protuberances on the end of its snout that may help it detect prey by touch. These completely aquatic snakes live in slow-moving streams where, anchored by their tails to submerged twigs or plants, they hang in the current and seize passing fish. From Australia and New Guinea, the two species of bockadams (*Cerberus*) are nocturnal snakes that inhabit estuaries and hunt mainly for mudskippers on mud flats exposed at low tide, while another estuarine species found over much of the Australo-Papuan region and also in Southeast Asia, the white-bellied mangrove snake (*Fordonia leucobelia*), feeds exclusively on crabs and other crustaceans. All homalopsines are viviparous.

Asian mudsnakes

A group of rather peculiar-looking snakes in the subfamily Xenoderminae have long bodies, distinctively enlarged heads, long tails, and, in some species, oddly-formed dorsal scales. The four genera and about 15 species are all restricted to Southeast Asia and Indonesia. Among the more widely distributed is the Javan mudsnake (*Xenodermis javanicus*), from Thailand, Malaysia, Java and Sumatra. This unusual little snake, only about 70 cm (27 in) long, has grain-shaped dorsal scales, with three rows of large, keeled tubercles, while on its lower sides the scales are triangular and separated by areas of bare skin. A frog-eater, it lives in wet leaf litter or waterlogged soil of tropical forests, swamps, marshes, and rice paddies, where for much of the time it leads a semi-aquatic and burrowing existence several centimetres below the surface.

TOP LEFT: *Oxyrhopus rhombifer*, a rear-fanged but only mildly venomous species from tropical South America. Compare with Spix's coral snake (p. 86), a venomous elapid found in the same region.

LEFT: A naturally-occurring colour mutation of the Mexican parrot snake, *Leptophis mexicanus*, from the Turneffe group of islands, Belize. Typical examples of this species are bright green with a bronze-coloured stripe on the back.

Asian reed snakes

Nine genera and about 50 species of reed snakes grouped in the subfamily Calamarinae are small – up to about 45 cm (1.5 ft) long – shiny-scaled snakes found mainly in Southeast Asia. They are adapted for burrowing, with slender, cylindrical bodies, fused head scales, and a rigidly constructed skull. If disturbed on the surface, they often wriggle down into the soil with remarkable speed. In both skin patterns and behaviour some are strikingly similar to certain highly venomous elapids. Pink-headed reed snakes (*Calamaria schlegeli*) for example, are deep bluish-black with a bright orange-red head, like both the Malayan long-glanded coral snake (*Maticora bivirgata*) and the red-headed krait (*Bungarus flaviceps*). Calamarines eat mostly earthworms and insect larvae, although the diet of some larger species, such as *Calamaria lumbricoidea*, also includes the lizards known as skinks. They are all egg-layers.

Snail-eating snakes, cat snakes and blunt-headed tree snakes

Snail-eating snakes

Three genera of colubrids from tropical America (*Dipsas*, *Sibon*, and *Sibynomorphus*) and one genus from Asia (*Pareas*) feed almost entirely on snails and slugs. These unusual snakes also resemble each other closely in appearance, though they appear to have arisen from independent origins and are grouped accordingly in separate subfamilies, the Dipsadinae and Pareatinae. The snake eats only the soft body of the snail inside the shell; grasping the body with its needle-like teeth, the snake extends its jaws alternately from side to side and continues advancing its grip in this way until the mollusc is dragged bodily from its shell. Two species of snail-eaters from Africa (*Duberria*) occasionally deal with larger snails by smashing their shells on the ground as some birds do, but these are unrelated to the Asian and New World forms.

Most snail-eating snakes are small – less than 1 m (3.3 ft) in length. The head is often large, with protruding eyes, and the snout usually short and blunt. The ringed snail-eater (*Sibon sartorii*) from Central America has a cylindrical body and is a terrestrial inhabitant of forest leaf litter, whereas the cloudy snail-eater (*S. nebulata*), short-faced snail-eater (*Dipsas brevifacies*) and most others are adapted for climbing, with long bodies flattened from side to side, and the head well differentiated from the slender neck. Many of them have no mental groove (a longitudinal groove under the chin found in almost all other snakes).

Cat and blunt-headed snakes

Among other species usually grouped in the Dipsadinae are six species of blunt-headed tree snakes (*Imantodes*). They are nocturnal and feed chiefly on small *Anolis* lizards, often plucking them from leaves and branches as they sleep. Similar, but more robustly built, are nine species of cat-eyed snakes (*Leptodeira*). These snakes often feed on a wide range of prey, including other snakes, although they are mostly frog-eaters. The small-spotted cat-eyed snake

OPPOSITE: **Malayan slug-eating snake, *Pareas vertebralis*. Slug and snail-eating snakes are generally small, secretive creatures and most are nocturnal. They locate prey by following the trails of mucus that slugs and snails leave behind as they move about.**

A large and formidable species that ranges into Mediterranean Europe is the Montpellier snake (*Malpolon monspessulanus*), a 1.8 m (6 ft) long steel-grey snake with strongly pronounced brows above its eyes that give it a fearsome appearance. More than 20 species of sand snakes (*Psammophis*) and three of skaapstekers (*Psammophylax*) are essentially African in distribution, with one species (*Psammophis condanarus*) in southeastern Asia and another (*P. lineolatus*) ranging into western China. On a drop-for-drop basis some species have relatively potent venoms, although the quantity expelled is normally too small to cause humans serious illness. Bites from link-marked sand snakes (*P. biseriatus*) and spotted skaapstekers (*Psammophylax rhombeatus*), however, have occasionally resulted in severe poisoning.

(*L. septentrionalis*) eats the egg masses of leaf-breeding tree frogs, to which they may be attracted by the vibrations generated by the loud calls of breeding frogs. Another subgroup of dipsadines, including *Adelphicos*, *Geophis*, and several other New World genera, live mostly underground, chiefly on a diet of earthworms.

ABOVE: **Yellow blunt-headed tree snake, *Imantodes inornatus*. The slender, laterally compressed body, long tail, and large eyes with vertically-elliptic pupils are characteristic of a species that lives in trees and hunts by night.**

Sand snakes, skaapstekers, bark snakes and beaked snakes

An example of one of the better defined subfamily divisions within the Colubridae is the Psammophiini, which includes seven genera of rear-fanged, mostly slender whip-like snakes from Africa, Mediterranean Europe, and Asia. They have large eyes and prey mostly on lizards and small rodents by sight, often hunting them down at great speed.

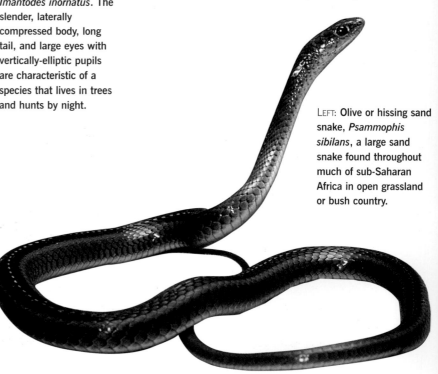

LEFT: **Olive or hissing sand snake, *Psammophis sibilans*, a large sand snake found throughout much of sub-Saharan Africa in open grassland or bush country.**

Other psammophines from Africa include two species of bark snakes (*Hemirhagerrhis*), which are small and rather secretive tree-dwellers, and four species of terrestrial beaked snakes (*Rhamphiophis*), named for their sharply-angled snouts.

Montpellier snakes and some sand snakes have the habit of smearing themselves with a colourless liquid secreted from glands in the snout, especially after sloughing or feeding. The precise function of this is not entirely clear, but since these snakes often live in dry, sun-scorched areas and are sometimes active even during the heat of midday, it may help prevent water loss.

African house snakes and file snakes

Of perhaps a dozen or more genera that may be assigned to the subfamily Boodontini, 15 species of African house snakes (*Lamprophis*) are small, 60-90 cm (2–3 ft) long, nocturnal constricting snakes that feed mainly on rodents and lizards. With smooth, shiny body scales in numerous rows, fairly short tails, and eyes with vertically elliptic pupils, they look rather like hatchling pythons, although differ in skin pattern. They often visit buildings in search of prey and are useful in controlling vermin.

Ten species of African file snakes (*Mehelya*), unrelated to Australasian file snakes, eat mainly snakes, including venomous species such as night adders and cobras, although they will also consume lizards, toads, and other ectothermic animals. Their common name alludes to the shape of the body, which is triangular in cross-section and resembles a three-cornered file, the abdomen being rather flat and the spine raised into a prominent ridge. The body scales of these snakes are heavily keeled and, unlike those of most colubrids, are contiguous rather than overlapping. In common with other boodontines, they are egg-layers.

Mussuranas, false pit vipers and neotropical water snakes

A diverse group of mostly South American colubrids currently placed in the subfamily Xenodontinae includes eight species of mussuranas (genus *Clelia*), renowned for their capacity to overpower and eat venomous pit vipers. Some undergo a striking colour change with age. Juveniles are bright orange-red with a black head and pale neck ring, but

BELOW: Mussurana, *Clelia clelia*, a powerful 2.5m (8ft) long Neotropical species that frequently predates on venomous snakes and is largely immune to the highly toxic venom of pit vipers.

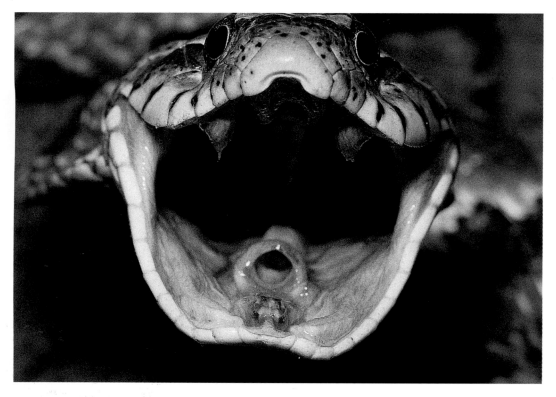

LEFT: **False pit viper,** *Waglerophis merremi*. **The enlarged fangs of this opisthoglyphous species can be seen in the rear of its mouth. Note also the extensive mouth cavity and forward-placed opening of the windpipe, modifications that enable snakes to swallow large prey.**

when they reach about 60 cm (2 ft) in length they gradually darken, and with successive moults of the skin eventually change to a uniform deep bluish-black.

Seven species of false pit vipers (*Waglerophis* and *Xenodon*) have colour patterns strikingly similar to those of some pit vipers; when provoked, these toad-eating snakes recoil and hiss loudly, as many pit vipers do, and also flatten their necks. Other South American xenodontines include over a dozen species of Neotropical water snakes (*Helicops*), two species of false water cobras (*Hydrodynastes*), and almost 20 of fast-moving racer-like snakes in the genus *Philodryas*. A nocturnal species from Brazil, *Tropidodryas striaticeps*, is unusual among colubrids in having a prehensile tail and using its tip as a lure to attract prey.

Dangerous colubrids

Many colubrids have enlarged fangs in the rear of the mouth and subdue prey by injecting venom. Biologists have always known about these species but until just over 40 years ago it was believed that all of them were generally harmless. The death in 1957, however, of a prominent herpetologist following the bite of a boomslang (*Dispholidus typus*), set alarm bells ringing that changed this view almost overnight and have echoed throughout the herpetological world ever since.

Many individuals who have experienced the effects of boomslang poisoning as well as the venoms of other dangerous African species such as cobras have remarked that, by comparison, the bite of the boomslang is by far the most painful and distressing. Among the worst of its extremely unpleasant symptoms is profuse internal bleeding; victims may need to be given 3.4 l (6 pt) or more of blood to replace that lost. The boomslang is generally an inoffensive snake that tends not to bite unless it is seriously provoked, but its venom is evidently highly toxic and perhaps even in the same league as that of some deadly elapids. Remarking on which of Africa's many dangerous snakes he considered the most venomous, Richard M. Isemonger, a distinguished African herpetologist and author of several books on snakes, placed the boomslang right at the top, above even the infamous mambas (*Dendroaspis*).

Bites from various other rear-fanged colubrids are also known to be lethally dangerous. In particular, those of African twig snakes (*Thelotornis*) have caused several fatalities, including the death in 1972 of an eminent German herpetologist, Robert Mertens, and more recently, several deaths have resulted from bites inflicted by an Asian species of keelback, the yamakagashi (*Rhabdophis tigrina*). Other species that appear to have unusually toxic venoms include the Central American road guarder (*Conophis lineatus*), Asian cat snakes (*Boiga*), and some Neotropical racers, particularly those of the genus *Philodryas*.

RIGHT: **Boomslang (*Dispholidus typus*) in characteristic defence posture. Boomslangs are widely distributed throughout much of Africa, and are entirely arboreal in habits. They feed mainly on small birds and lizards, especially chameleons.**

Cobras, Coral Snakes, Kraits, Taipans and Sea Snakes
Family *Elapidae*

The Elapidae is a diverse family of venomous snakes, and includes some of the largest and most formidable species known. Various elapids, such as the coral snakes, kraits, and some sea snakes, are also among the most spectacularly coloured. As a group, the 65 genera and 300 or so species are characterized by enlarged, non-erectile fangs in the front of the mouth (see p. 8), which fit into grooved slots in the lower jaw when the mouth is closed, and they have a venom that is predominantly neurotoxic (see p. 17). Elapids also lack a loreal scale (on the side of the snout between the nostril and eye), a feature that otherwise characterizes only the burrowing asps and a few small colubrids. They occur in all of the warmer regions of the world except Madagascar, and are particularly well represented in Australia, where they reach their greatest diversity and outnumber all other kinds of snakes.

Diversification of elapid snakes

Most elapids are ground-dwellers, notable exceptions being the arboreal mambas (*Dendroaspis*) and tree cobras (*Pseudohaje*), and the aquatic water cobras (*Boulengerina*), all of which occur in Africa. The family also includes many sea-living species, the sea snakes, which, although different in habits and some features of anatomy, are nonetheless closely related. Their distinctive appearance is the result of adaptive modifications made necessary for living in the sea, rather than separate ancestry. They are almost exclusively marine and, except for a few species that come ashore for a short time to breed and lay eggs, most never venture onto dry land.

Apart from one genus of especially stout, viper-like terrestrial species, elapids are all comparatively slender in build. Many have the appearance of harmless colubrids, and in some this similarity extends also to coloration; the red-yellow-and-black-banded coral snakes of the Americas, for example, bear striking resemblance to various 'mimic' species found in the same areas of distribution (see p. 81). Herpetologists have traditionally recognized several subfamilies of elapid snakes, but do not fully understand

BELOW: **Although undoubtedly a very dangerous snake, the hammadryad or king cobra, *Ophiophagus hannah*, prefers to escape unless it is provoked. This is not true of nesting females, however, which may attack without provocation.**

Venomous or harmless?

Among the most remarkable features of snakes is the strikingly similar appearance that some harmless types have to certain venomous species. This apparent 'mimicry' appears to have arisen primarily to escape predation, and its survival value is clear. The New World coral snakes, for example, advertise their noxious character with a pattern of red, yellow, and black rings that say 'Stop! Danger!', and this livery of aposematic (warning) colours is imitated by no fewer than 115 other species – about 18% of all American snakes. One of the most impressive of all mimics is the harlequin snake (*Urotheca elapoides*), a colubrid from Central America, which is known to imitate several different species of coral snake throughout its range and also even their locally-specific colour variants.

It is not only other snakes that appear to have adopted mimicry as a means of evading predators. Certain kinds of sea-living eels are similar in coloration to the venomous sea kraits (*Laticauda*), and a striking mimic of the eyelash palm pit viper (*Bothriechis schlegelii*) from tropical America exists in the unlikely form of a caterpillar. *Hemeroplanes triptolemus* is a species of hawk moth found throughout much of the eyelash viper's range, and the final stage of its larva bears an extraordinary resemblance to this pit viper. At rest it resembles a twig, but when alarmed it turns its forebody upside down, withdraws its legs into the body cavity, and expands the thorax into a remarkably lifelike impersonation of an eyelash viper's head. The whole transformation is completed in just a few seconds. The third and fourth larval stages of *Hemeroplanes* are said to mimic a different snake, the brown vine snake, *Oxybelis aeneus*.

LEFT: **Spix's coral snake, *M. spixii* (near right) and one of its harmless mimics, *Simophis rhinostoma* (far left) (see also p. 23).**

evolutionary patterns within this large and complex group. With this in mind, they are grouped here under informal headings that reflect some of their shared features but not necessarily any particular evolutionary relationship.

Cobras, mambas, and other Afro-Asian elapids

Cobras and their relatives are distributed throughout much of Africa and Asia. Some grow to considerable lengths. At an adult length of 5 m (16.4 ft), the hamadryad or king cobra (*Ophiophagus hannah*), is the world's largest venomous snake, while among 18 species of 'typical' cobras (genus *Naja*), the forest cobra (*N. melanoleuca*) may occasionally exceed 3 m (10 ft), and several others reach lengths of 2.5 m (8.2 ft). A feature for which cobras are especially noted is their ability to spread the skin of their necks into a flattened hood. Several cobras also have fangs specially modified for the purposes of 'squirting' venom (see p. 84). Except for the ringhals (*Hemachatus haemachatus*), a viviparous species from Africa, all of them lay

BELOW: **Egyptian cobra, *Naja haje.***

ABOVE: **Red spitting cobra,** *Naja pallida,* **from northeastern Africa. When at rest or on the move, the hood of cobras lies collapsed along the sides of the neck as rather loose skin.**

OPPOSITE: **Caterpillar of** *Hemeroplanes triptolemus* **mimicking a palm pit viper,** *Bothriechis schlegelii* **(inset). If molested, the caterpillar will even behave in the same defensive manner as a viper, reacting with quick, sideways-directed 'strikes'.**

eggs, and the females of at least some species also stay with their clutches throughout incubation. Female king cobras (*Ophiophagus hannah*) take particular care of their eggs by laying them in a nest they build from leaves, often deep inside bamboo thickets, and watching over them until they hatch.

The Mambas

Probably the most feared group of elapids are the mambas (*Dendroaspis*), which occur only in Africa south of the Sahara. There are four species, of which the black mamba (*D. polylepis*) in particular is infamous for its speed of movement, unpredictable disposition, and unusually toxic venom. Brownish in colour, it is mostly terrestrial, whereas the three remaining forms are predominantly green and live in trees. Mambas (from a Zulu word meaning 'big snake'), are large, slender, agile snakes. The black mamba may attain lengths of up to 4.3 m (14 ft) and is extremely fast in its movements: across open ground it has been recorded traveling at speeds of 15 km/h (9 mph), and on downhill slopes is almost certainly capable of moving even faster. The neurotoxic venom of black mambas is fast-acting and can be life-threatening within minutes. Just two drops are considered a fatal dose in humans, and with each bite these snakes are capable of injecting up to 20 drops! Like cobras, they are able to flatten the neck, although not nearly to the extent of forming a distinct hood.

Defensive specializations of cobras

Perhaps no other venomous snakes are more instantly recognizable than the cobras. With its head raised high and neck spread into a flattened 'hood', the appearance of one of these animals primed to defend itself is an unnerving sight, and surely one of the most menacing spectacles in nature.

All cobras are capable of spreading a hood, which they achieve by extending the specially lengthened ribs of the neck. They normally resort to this behaviour, however, only when threatened. In some species, such as the ringhals (*Hemachatus haemachatus*) and most African species of the genus Naja, the hood is marked on the underside with contrasting dark cross-bars, whereas the monocled cobra (*N. kaouthia*) and other Asian species have a single or double eye-like marking on the dorsal surface that is revealed as the hood is spread.

Several species of cobra also defend themselves by 'squirting' venom. The fangs of these species have an orifice on the anterior surface rather than at the tip, through which venom is forced at high pressure and directed at an enemy in a well-aimed stream, usually at the eyes and face. In certain African species the fangs also have spiral grooves inside that function much like the rifling of a gun barrel, helping to fine-tune the accuracy of the 'spit', as it has become misleadingly known. When 'spitting', the cobra raises its neck well off the ground and tilts its head upwards, holding its jaws widely agape. By curling back the upper lip just enough to expose the orifice of the fang, however, some species can spit with the mouth only partially open, enabling them to perform this feat from almost any position. The effective range to which the venom can be ejected varies between species, but in the larger ones, such as the black-necked spitting cobra (*Naja nigricollis*), it can be as much as 3 m (10 ft). On contact with the eyes it causes pain and almost instant blindness, and if left too long before being washed out some permanent loss of sight may result.

Should their hooded threat posture or 'spitting' fail to deter an adversary, some cobra species will, if molested, resort to feigning death, and this extraordinary behaviour can be very convincing. The ringhals, for example, turns over on its side and becomes limp and lifeless with its mouth agape and tongue hanging out, and may continue to act in this way even if it is picked up. Most cobras will also hiss loudly if threatened, and in the king cobra (*Ophiophagus hannah*) this may take the form of an unusual 'growling' sound.

LEFT: **Venomous snakes are capable of delivering a dangerous bite virtually from the moment of birth. Only minutes old, this newly hatched red spitting cobra, *Naja pallida*, is able to defend itself also by spraying venom at an enemy's eyes.**

Other Old World elapids

Other African elapids include two species of aquatic cobras (*Boulengerina*), restricted to the vicinity of large lakes. Their bodies are thick and heavy, and the neck can be flattened into a hood, although not to the extent seen in typical cobras. Much of their time is spent diving for fish, their principal food, and they may remain submerged for long periods at a time, but they are also to some extent terrestrial and when not in the water lie in crevices among rocks near the shoreline or bask in the sun. They grow to a length of about 2.4 m (8 ft). Two species of shield-nosed cobras (*Aspidelaps*) are 50–70 cm (20–28 in) long, stout-bodied snakes that have modified snouts for burrowing through soil and rooting out their prey, mainly frogs and lizards. Both species spread a narrow hood and hiss loudly when alarmed. Also from Africa are two species of tree cobra (*Pseudohaje*), large, slender, snakes with enormous eyes and long tails, and a small, little-known burrowing species, *Paranaja multifasciata*; all three are almost hoodless.

Two other genera of cobra-like snakes occur in the Afro-Asian region, and the relationships of these to other Old World elapids is less well defined. The desert black snake (*Walterinnesia aegyptia*) is a 1 m (3.3 ft) long nocturnal species found in arid habitats of the Middle East, while the other genus contains eight mostly small, burrowing species of garter snakes (*Elapsoidea*) in various parts of Africa.

The black mamba occurs throughout the eastern half of tropical Africa, favouring dry open bush country and living in abandoned animal holes, hollow trees, or termite mounds. An individual may often take up residence in such a chosen lair for several weeks or even months. They hunt during the day, mostly for bush babies, hyraxes, and gerbils, and other small mammals, although they have also been observed to eat sugarbirds, snapping them out of the air as the birds hover around flowers, feeding on nectar. In pursuit of prey they may descend underground into rodent burrows and climb high into trees. Black mambas are only 38–61 cm (15–24 in) long when they hatch but grow rapidly: some may reach a length of 1.8 m (6 ft) before they are a year old.

ABOVE: **Black mamba, *Dendroaspis polylepis*. The common name of this fearsome snake alludes not to the colour of the body, which is uniform leaden-grey or olive brown, but to the purplish-black lining of the mouth.**

New World coral snakes

These snakes are best known for their often vivid, red-yellow-and-black-banded colour patterns, which serve as warning signals alerting potential predators to their dangerous character – many animals that eat snakes, particularly birds of prey, appear to have an innate aversion to such markings and instinctively avoid them. There are three genera, *Leptomicrurus* (with three species), *Micruroides* (one species), and *Micrurus* (62 species), and almost all of them are similar in appearance. The numbers of scale rows on the body and the arrangement of scales on the head are constant, and their colour patterns tend also to be very similar. Most are confined in distribution to tropical forests, although one species, the harlequin coral snake (*M. fulvius*) occurs in southern USA, and the Sechura coral snake (*M. tschudii*) and Sonoran coral snake (*Micruroides euryxanthus*) are desert species. They are typically rather slender snakes, with heads scarcely wider than their bodies, short tails, and small eyes, and most are strikingly marked with a pattern of red, yellow and black rings; exceptions include the white-banded coral snake (*M. albicinctus*) from the lowland forests of Brazil, a predominantly black species with contrasting rings of white spots, and the Andean black-backed coral snake (*Leptomicrurus narducci*), characterized by a uniformly dark-coloured body and a red- or yellow-spotted abdomen.

New World coral snakes all have a specialized diet, consisting mostly of other snakes, including their own species. Allen's coral snake (*Micrurus alleni*) from southern Central America also eats swamp eels, while the diet of the Surinam coral snake (*M. surinamensis*) consists almost exclusively of these and various other fish. Hemprich's coral snake (*M. hemprichii*) from northern South America is particularly unusual in eating only onycophorans, small invertebrates that look like a cross between an earthworm and a caterpillar. Coral snakes are all active foragers and, while some appear to be generally nocturnal, others have no particular set pattern of activity.

The bites of New World coral snakes are dangerous and perhaps only the small Sonoran coral snake (*Micruroides euryxanthus*), which produces little more than 6 mg (0.0002 oz) of a relatively weak venom, is not deadly to humans. They have rather short fangs and their mouths are relatively small, which has given rise to the myth that these snakes are incapable of biting humans unless they happen to fasten on to a thin piece of skin, such as that between the fingers. Actually, even the smallest species have a surprisingly wide gape and are able to deliver a bite to almost any part of the body.

RIGHT: **Spix's coral snake,** *Micrurus spixii*, **from Amazonian South America is one of the largest species of** *Micrurus*, **with adults reaching lengths of 1.6 m (5 ft). Compare with** *Oxyrhopus rhombifer* **(p. 73).**

A reproductive success story – the short-tailed coral snake

Coral snakes usually lay their eggs in leaf litter, beneath rotten logs, or in other places similarly conducive to incubation. The short-tailed coral snake (*Micrurus frontalis*) in Uruguay, however, has found a particularly novel way of taking care of its eggs and ensuring that they are provided with optimum conditions. It lays its clutch of one to seven eggs in the nest mound of a particular species of ant, *Acromyrex lobicornis* – specifically in that part of the nest used by the ants for cultivating a fungus on which they feed. In this underground chamber, the humidity remains more or less constant, and the temperature varies by little more than 2°C (3.6°F), providing an ideal incubation

LEFT: **Short-tailed coral snake, *Micrurus frontalis*, with tail raised in typical defence display.**

environment for the developing eggs. The ants also clean the eggs, reducing the risk of them becoming contaminated by bacteria or mould, and will even protect them from attack by predatory insects. It is not entirely clear how or indeed if the ants benefit reciprocally from this behaviour, but it may be that the newly-hatched coral snakes provide some protection by feeding on amphisbaenians (burrowing, legless, snake-like reptiles) and blind snakes, which are natural predators of ants and often invade their nests.

Other snakes are known to use anthills and also termite nests for incubating their eggs, among which the Patagonian green snake (*Philodryas patagonensis*) may often lay its eggs in the same ant nests as those used by short-tailed coral snakes.

ABOVE: **Malayan long-glanded or blue coral snake, *Maticora bivirgata*. This spectacularly coloured species occurs throughout much of Southeast Asia and Indonesia. It is nocturnal and highly secretive.**

Asian coral snakes and kraits

Asian coral snakes appear to be closely related to the New World forms and, like these species, many have vivid colour patterns. Two species of *Maticora* from Southeast Asia are particularly brightly coloured; the blue Malayan long-glanded coral snake (*M. bivirgata*) (left) and the banded coral snake (*M. intestinalis*) which is brownish with a red or orange dorsal stripe enclosed between two black stripes. The venom glands of these species are especially large, extending under the skin for about one-third the length of the body. In common with most New World coral snakes, they feed on other snakes, and are egg-layers. Eleven other coral-snake-like species grouped in the genus *Calliophis* occur over much of Asia, including India and Sri Lanka, southern China, Japan, and the Philippines. These are small species with exceptionally slender bodies and small heads and eyes. They are nocturnal and feed mostly on other reptiles, especially snakes.

Similar to the Asian coral snakes in appearance, although somewhat larger, are the 12 species of kraits (*Bungarus*). Kraits occur over much the same range as Asian coral snakes, and like them also feed chiefly on other snakes. An exception is the many-banded krait (*B. multicinctus*), which eats mainly fish. Most have an enlarged mid-dorsal row of scales and peculiar protrusions on the vertebrae, the precise function of which has not been established but may play some defensive role in body thrashing, to which these snakes often resort when molested. As with coral snakes, some are brightly coloured.

ABOVE: **Banded krait,** *Bungarus fasciatus.* **This species is among the largest of kraits, with adults reaching lengths over 2 m (6.6 ft).**

Terrestrial elapids of the Australo-Papuan region

The greatest number of elapid snakes are found in the area of Australia and New Guinea (the Australo-Papuan region), where in places they are the dominant species. In mainland Australia alone there are over 80 different kinds, compared to some 60 of all four other families that occur there put together. Almost all are terrestrial, and of the few species that occasionally climb, none show any clear specializations for arboreal life. Quite why there should be so few elapids in the Australo-Papuan region that live in trees, where this habitat is otherwise exploited only by a few pythons and colubrids, is puzzling, but it is interesting that their nearest relatives in Southeast Asia are also mostly terrestrial. Perhaps a suitable opportunity for diversification among these forms has never arisen or their ancestral relatives had little natural inclination to climb, but this does not seem to be the complete story.

Taipans, brown snakes, and whip snakes

The terrestrial elapids of Australia and the New Guinea region comprise two principal groups, one of which includes mostly egg-laying species with a paired row of scales beneath the tail, and the other is viviparous with a single row of subcaudal scales. Notable among the larger egg-laying forms, two species of taipans (*Oxyuranus*) are arguably the most fast-moving, unpredictable, and dangerously venomous of all Australo-Papuan elapids. Drop-for-drop, the venom of the inland taipan (*O. microlepidotus*) is more toxic than that of any other snake in the world. This species is associated primarily with the flat plains of southwestern Queensland. Related to the taipans are six species of *Pseudechis* and seven of *Pseudonaja*, known variously as 'brown snakes' or 'black snakes' in allusion to their predominant body colour. Among the most widespread, both in Australia and possibly also New Guinea, is the mulga or king brown snake (*Pseudechis australis*), a formidable 2.5 m (8 ft) long species that is often unperturbed in the presence of humans, and reluctant to move away when encountered. All are dangerous and, if provoked, some are highly aggressive. A large New Guinea species, the Papuan black snake (*Pseudechis papuanus*), is reputed to attack with a tenacity unrivalled by any other species, a reputation which has earned it the local name of auguma (meaning 'to bite again'). Brown snakes and black snakes feed on frogs, lizards, small mammals and occasionally birds, and like many elapids in this region, often constrict their prey as well as injecting venom.

With long slender bodies, eight species of whip snakes (*Demansia*) are among the most agile of all Australo-Papuan elapids. Though normally day-active, they may also be active at night when the weather is warm. Although all are venomous, only large specimens are regarded as dangerous to humans.

Tiger snakes, death adders, and other live-bearers

Live-bearing is uncommon among terrestrial elapids. In Africa and Asia, only the ringhals (*Hemachatus haemachatus*) and perhaps one or two other species produce offspring by this means, while in tropical America elapids are exclusively oviparous. In Australian elapids, however, live-bearing is more prevalent, especially among species found in the cooler, southern part of the continent, and some kinds have relatively large numbers of offspring. The litters of the two species of tiger snakes (*Notechis*) in particular may sometimes contain more than 40, and a female black tiger snake (*N. ater*) from Tasmania once even gave birth to 109 babies, more than has been recorded in any Australian snake. Tiger snakes are large, up to 2.5 m (8 ft) long, stocky species widely distributed in southern Australia, and black tiger snakes also occur on many of the offshore islands, often in huge numbers. Males appear to be much stronger than

BELOW: **The most formidable of all Australian-Papuan elapids, the taipan, *Oxyuranus scutellatus*, is also the largest venomous snake in this region. There are authenticated records of examples up to 4 m (13 ft).**

TOP: **Tiger snake,** *Notechis scutatus.*

BOTTOM: **Common death adder,** *Acanthophis antarcticus.* **Death adders are elapids that resemble and behave like vipers. In their native Australia and New Guinea, where there are no vipers, these snakes occupy the same ecological role.**

females of the same body size, perhaps because of the strength needed during bouts of ritual male-to-male combat, or because females need to store more fat for reproduction. Also among the largest of Australia's live-bearing elapids are three species of copperhead (*Austrelaps*). Like the tiger snakes, they are more resistant to cold than most other species and can sometimes be found sun-bathing even in the freezing conditions of winter.

A group of ten highly dangerous live-bearing species from Australia and New Guinea that are extremely well camouflaged, and have venoms of exceptional potency, are

the death adders (*Acanthophis*). Whereas virtually all other elapids are rather slender snakes that actively hunt for their prey, these are sedentary, particularly heavy-set snakes that burrow under leaf litter and lie in wait for small animals to pass within striking distance. As a consequence, they are often difficult to see, and in places represent a serious risk of snakebite – fatal accidents attributed to these snakes are reported each year. Their home ranges may be smaller than those of any other elapids, and within an area of only a few square metres they may not move around very much for weeks at a time. Another small adder-like elapid, the bardick (*Brachyaspis curta*) is an exclusively Australian species that feeds mostly on frogs and also uses a 'sit-and-wait' hunting technique.

Three species of broad-headed snakes (*Hoplocephalus*) are slender, nocturnal species and the only elapids in Australia that are regularly arboreal. They feed principally on lizards, but occasionally eat frogs and mammals. A jet-black snake dotted with yellow scales, *H. bungaroides* from southeastern districts is a particularly spectacular species confined mostly to rocky sandstone habitats, where its survival is under threat from commercial 'bushrock' collectors. Now classed as endangered, at the time of European settlement during the 19th century this beautiful snake was common even in the centre of Sydney.

Australian coral snakes, crowned snakes, and forest snakes

Several genera of small, mostly egg-laying elapids in Australia and New Guinea are noted for their burrowing habits, defensive displays, and unusual diets. These include 13 species of Australian coral snakes (*Simoselaps*), which are variously marked with red-and-black or yellow-and-black bands and have a specialized diet consisting almost wholly of reptile eggs. Unlike those of other elapids, the teeth on the pterygoid bones in at least one species, the narrow-banded coral snake (*S. fasciatus*), are saw-like. The black-and-white-ringed bandy-bandy (*Vermicella annulata*) is a similarly patterned Australian snake and one of five species in this genus that eat mostly blind snakes. When alarmed, it assumes a curious defensive posture in which the body is elevated in large loops and twisted around, probably as a means of increasing the effectiveness of its black-and-white warning bands. The three species of Australian crowned snakes (*Cacophis*) and perhaps the three species of New Guinea crowned snakes (*Aspidomorphus*) also adopt unusual defensive postures if provoked; the dorsal coloration of these snakes is generally brownish, but the head and neck are more boldly marked with a white or yellowish stripe, and when danger threatens the snakes arch their forebodies off the ground but keep the head pointing directly downwards, thus displaying the colourful head markings to their full effect. Nine species of forest snakes (*Toxicocalamus*), all of which occur only in New Guinea, are among the very few elapids that feed on invertebrates. Earthworms comprise a large proportion of their diets, but they may also eat fly pupae and small snails. They are small, secretive snakes and live almost entirely underground.

Small-eyed snakes, Indonesian coral snakes, and the Fijiian bola

Although relatively close to Australia in geographical terms, New Guinea, the Solomon Islands and Fiji have a number of elapid snakes that occur only in these areas and are quite distinctive. During the day, the New Guinea small eyed-snake (*Micropechis ikaheka*) shelters beneath leaf litter and other forest floor debris, or in the coconut plantation beneath the discarded heaps of coconut husks in plantation areas, where it poses a serious danger to local workers. This essentially banded species has an unusually pale coloration, a feature for which it has become known in parts of its native land as 'white snake'.

Similar to the small-eyed snake is *Loveridgelaps elapoides* from the Solomon Islands, a strikingly marked black-and-white-banded species with patches of bright yellow on its back. This rare, nocturnal elapid occurs mostly near forest streams and feeds on frogs,

BELOW: **Australian banded snake,** *Simoselaps littoralis*.

ABOVE: **The small-eyed snake,** *Micropechis ikaheka*, **is a fairly large – up to 1.5 m (5 ft) long – species endemic to New Guinea, where it is a nocturnal inhabitant of monsoon forests and also occurs in coconut plantations.**

OPPOSITE PAGE: **Yellow-lipped sea krait,** *Laticauda colubrina*.

a habit it shares with another endemic, diurnal species, *Salomonelaps* par. From the island of Bougainville near New Guinea, Hediger's coral snake, *Parapistocalamus hedigeri*, is a small elapid, up to 50 cm (20 in) long, about which very little is known, other than it is a nocturnal, semi-burrowing form that may feed on the eggs of large land snails. Perhaps an even more poorly understood species is the Fijiian ground snake, or bola (*Ogmodon vittatus*). This snake has one of the most isolated distributions of any elapid in the region, occurring only on the small island of Vitu Levu nearly 2000 km (1240 miles) from its nearest relatives in the Solomons. Its known distribution appears to be further limited to two adjacent watersheds in the southeastern

part of this island. A diminutive burrowing species, only about 20 cm (8 in) long, it is found in forest soils of inland mountain valleys, and eats mainly earthworms.

Marine elapids – the 'sea snakes'

Perhaps the most intriguing of all snakes, in terms of their origins, relationships, and specialized life habits, are the sea snakes. The 60 or so species include some of the most completely aquatic of all air-breathing vertebrates, and except for one that is endemic to a single freshwater lake in the Philippine Islands, and two that inhabit a brackish lagoon on Rennell Island in the Solomons, they are exclusively marine. Herpetologists once thought that all sea-living snakes represented a single, divergent line of evolution, but the weight of evidence now available suggests fairly conclusively that there are at least two principal groups, the sea kraits and the true sea snakes, which both arose within the Elapidae and evolved independently from different mainland ancestors.

The sea kraits probably arose within the Asian radiation of elapids, or possibly from a very early Australian species. These snakes are egg-layers and come ashore to breed. The 'true' sea snakes appear to be of Australian origin, and are more highly specialized than sea kraits. They are live-bearers, and while a few species may occasionally haul themselves out on to rocks or exposed reefs to sun themselves, most never leave the water.

Marine elapids are found in all tropical seas, but are absent from the Caribbean and the Atlantic Ocean. They are essentially creatures of Asian and Australian coastal waters, with only a few species ranging well out to sea. In fact only one species, the yellow-bellied sea snake (*Pelamis platurus*) is truly ocean-going. At times, people have seen large aggregations of certain species floating on the surface of the sea – on one such occasion, in 1932, passengers aboard a steamer passing through the Strait of Malacca off Malaysia, reported seeing what must have been a phenomenal number of Stokes's sea snakes (*Astrotia stokesii*) all massed together in an enormous 'slick', which they said was about 3 m (10 ft) wide and extended for a distance of some 96 km (60 miles)!

Sea kraits

All five species of sea kraits are included within a single genus, *Laticauda*. As egg-layers, they are more tied to land than the live-bearing sea snakes. During the reproductive season they come ashore at night, often in huge numbers, on beaches, or in wooded areas at the juncture of water and land, with females often depositing their eggs communally in caves. At other times, especially after feeding, sea kraits may also crawl out onto logs floating in the sea or emergent rocks near the tide line to sun themselves. They have broad ventral scales, legacies of their terrestrial relatives, blue or yellow colour patterns banded with black, and reach a maximum size of about 2 m (6.6 ft). Most feed mainly on eels, which they locate by poking their heads into holes

or crevices, and once they have caught them, quickly swallow even relatively large prey. As with the freshwater file snakes (Family Acrochordidae), females are conspicuously larger than males. Females may also feed in shallower water and prey on different kinds of eels than their mates.

Sea kraits in particular are among the most heavily exploited of all snakes, and in certain parts of the world are a major source of livelihood. In Oriental countries they are widely eaten as delicacies, and in the Philippines and other parts of Southeast Asia vast numbers are harvested each year for the leather industry.

The true sea snakes

Although similar in overall appearance, the marine elapids of this group are more specialized for ocean life than the sea kraits. The 16 genera and 56 species are all viviparous, and spend their entire lives at sea. In length, they range from as little as 50 cm (20 in) in some species of reef sea snake (*Aipysurus*) to 2.75 m (9 ft) in the yellow sea snake (*Hydrophis spiralis*). The most massively built is Stoke's sea snake (*Astrotia stokesii*), which at an adult length of 2 m (6.6 ft) may have a midbody girth of over 26 cm (10 in). Three species of the genera *Ephalophis*, *Hydrelaps* and *Parahydrophis* have broad ventral scales and are relatively primitive forms restricted mostly to estuaries, while at the other end of the spectrum, the monotypic yellow-bellied sea snake (*Pelamis platurus*) is a highly adapted, oceanic species with a geographic range greater than that of any snake. This species, uniquely marked with a pattern of yellow and black stripes, is found across the Pacific as far west as the western coasts of Central and South America, and as far south as New Zealand and the Cape of

BELOW: **Elegant sea snake, *Hydrophis elegans*, a species from coastal regions of western New Guinea and northern Australia. Note the paddle-like tail for swimming.**

Good Hope. It occurs mainly in the narrow strips of calm water where two ocean currents meet, feeding on small fish that congregate around the accumulations of seaweed debris often found floating in these areas.

Adaptive modifications of marine elapids

- The body is flattened from side to side. Stokes's sea snake (*Astrotia stokesii*), a large and unusually stout-bodied species, has a midventral pair of scales enlarged to form a longitudinal keel on its abdomen which probably acts as a stabilizer.
- Some species have unusually small heads and narrow necks in relation to their otherwise stout bodies, which enables them to reach deep into holes and crevices to seize their prey.
- All species have flattened, paddle-like tails with which to propel the body when swimming; in the more highly modified sea snakes, this structure is supported by elongated neural spines on the tail vertebrae. Olive sea snakes (*Aipysurus laevis*) and perhaps other nocturnal species have photoreceptors (light-sensitive organs) on the tail, which they use to ensure that this end of the body is not left exposed when hiding among crevices during the day.
- The single lung is longer than that of most other snakes (enabling them to stay underwater longer), and stored air can be pumped forward when needed into the vascular part to sustain respiration. Most species are active at depths of less than about 30 m (100 ft), although some may occasionally dive to about 150 m (500 ft) or more. They can stay underwater for at least 30 minutes.
- The nostrils are equipped with valves to keep out sea water. In sea kraits (*Laticauda*) the nostrils are placed on the side of the snout, while in sea snakes they are on the top.
- A modified rostral scale (or in some species an extension of tissue behind this scale) that fits into a notch at the front of the lower jaw seals the opening through which the tongue is normally protruded while the snake is underwater.
- A special salt excretion gland beneath the tongue enables marine elapids to rid themselves of excessive salt. The skin of these snakes is also more impermeable to salt than that of their terrestrial relatives.
- Sea kraits and sea snakes shed their skin more frequently than do terrestrial species, at intervals of 2-6 weeks. This may have some effect in helping to keep the body free of barnacles and other small marine organisms.

The venom of most marine elapids, although produced only in relatively small amounts, is powerfully neurotoxic (see p. 17). That of some species also contains myotoxins, which destroy muscle cells. Sea kraits tend to be docile and may even be handled with little risk of being bitten, whereas some sea snakes bite readily. The beaked sea snake (*Enhydrina schistosa*) in particular appears to be more aggressive than most and is suspected of being responsible for many deaths among Malaysian fisherman.

Fish form the staple diet of most marine elapids, and some species specialize in feeding on particular kinds. Sea kraits (*Laticauda*), for example, hunt for eels among coral reefs, including potentially dangerous moray eels, which they usually release following the initial strike and leave for the venom to take effect before attempting to consume, while beaked sea snakes (*Enhydrina schistosa*) forage along the muddy bottom of estuaries for catfish. The diet of some species, such as the olive sea snake (*Aipysurus laevis*), also includes crabs and other crustaceans, while others eat only fish eggs. White-spotted sea snakes (*Aipysurus eydouxi*) and turtle-headed sea snakes (*Emydocephalus annulatus*) scrape fish eggs off rocks using enlarged labial scales, and it has been suggested that these species also 'suck' out the buried eggs of gobbies, blennies and other bottom-dwelling fish, using a special muscle in the floor of their mouths. They have a degenerate venom apparatus and their venom is also relatively weak.

Sea kraits and sea snakes tend to produce smaller clutches and litters than do their terrestrial relatives. Some species, such as the viperine sea snake (*Praescutata viperina*), produce small litters of three to four relatively large young, whereas others give birth to larger numbers of smaller offspring.

ABOVE: *Aipysurus duboisii*, a large species of reef sea snake from the Timor Sea and coastal regions of northern and western Australia.

Vipers
Family *Viperidae*

Vipers comprise a highly evolved family of snakes with a characteristic venom-injecting apparatus that is more sophisticated than that found in any other group. Unlike mambas, coral snakes and other elapids, they have large, erectile fangs that are capable of being 'pivoted' independently of one another (see p. 8). Normally, these are kept folded back along the roof of the mouth, encased in a protective sheath of soft tissue (the vagina dentis), but are rotated forwards as the mouth is opened to strike. The fangs have enclosed venom canals and their large size enables vipers to inject venom deep into the tissues of their prey, where it is rapidly absorbed; in this respect the fangs can be compared with a hypodermic needle. A West African species, the Gaboon viper (*Bitis gabonica*), is credited with having the longest fangs of all, measuring almost 5 cm (2 in). Only the stiletto snakes (*Atractaspis*) have similarly large, front-mounted fangs that are hollow and capable of independent movement.

Vipers are usually characterized as heavy-bodied, terrestrial snakes, and adaptive radiation in this family has not been as extensive as in some others. With the exception of a few desert-dwelling forms that, by shuffling their bodies are able to 'sink' vertically into loose sand, none are habitual burrowers, and only one North American species, the cottonmouth (*Agkistrodon piscivorus*), is semi-aquatic.

LEFT: **With a scaly horn on the tip of its snout, the nose-horned viper, *Vipera ammodytes*, from the eastern Mediterranean region is one of the more distinctive European vipers. It is also one of the most venomous.**

BELOW: **Chinese white-lipped pit viper, *Trimeresurus albolabris*.**

There are, though, many tree-dwelling species that have relatively slender bodies with strongly prehensile tails.

The Viperidae has an almost worldwide distribution, and embraces four subfamilies: the Azemiopinae, with a single species, the night adders (Causinae), the 'true' vipers (Viperinae), and the pit vipers (Crotalinae). A Eurasian species, the common viper or adder (*Vipera berus*), has a particularly large range, including areas within the Arctic Circle, further north than any other snake. The snake with a range that extends further south than any other species is also a viper, the Patagonian lancehead (*Bothrops ammodytoides*).

Feeding habits of vipers

Vipers are among the greatest exponents of the 'sit-and-wait' hunting technique, and have evolved highly cryptic body markings that enable them to remain concealed from their predators and the animals on which they feed. Using chemical traces of their prey to seek out strategic ambush sites, they lie in wait for a meal to pass within striking reach, remaining motionless in the same place often for days or even weeks until either their patience is finally rewarded or instinct drives them to try elsewhere.

In some vipers the tip of the tail is coloured differently and used as a lure for attracting prey. Peringuey's adders (*Bitis peringueyi*) buried in desert sand, will wriggle their black-and-white-banded tail tips above the surface to attract foraging lizards. Similar behaviour is seen in some non-viperid snakes, such as the death adders (*Acanthophis*, Family Elapidae) from Australia and New Guinea.

The bite of a viper takes the form of a rapid 'stabbing' movement, for which the

ABOVE: **Mexican cantil, *Agkistrodon bilineatus*. Juveniles of this species have bright yellow tail-tips and flick them about in the manner of a wriggling worm to entice prey within striking range.**

BELOW: **Fea's viper, *Azemiops feae*, is the only representative of the subfamily Azemiopinae. A most unusually coloured snake, its pattern is unlike that of any other viper.**

fangs are fully erected and the mouth opened to almost 180° (see page 8). If the prey is small, the snake may restrain it in its mouth until the venom takes effect, but in most cases it withdraws its fangs immediately, and locates the dying animal afterwards by following its scent. Throughout the snake's life the fangs are continuously replaced by others that grow and move forward from behind; when the next-in-line is ready for use, the functioning fang loosens at its base and either falls out or is left embedded in the body of the snake's next meal. The venom of many vipers has a pronounced digestive effect on their prey, and this is believed to be a major contributory factor in the ability of some species to live in seasonally cold environments, where low temperatures may otherwise not permit effective digestion.

Fea's viper
Subfamily *Azemiopinae*

Fea's viper (*Azemiops feae*) is the only representative of the subfamily Azemiopinae. It is a rare species found only in the remote mountain cloud forests of southern and central China, Tibet, and Vietnam, and is widely regarded as the most primitive of all vipers. Although a true viper, it superficially resembles an elapid or colubrid snake in that

the top of its head is covered with large symmetrical plates. The body scales are all smooth, a feature it shares with only one other species, *Calloselasma rhodostoma*, a pit viper from Southeast Asia. Little is known about the natural history of *Azemiops*, other than it is a ground-dwelling, oviparous snake that feeds on shrews and perhaps other small rodents. Like pit vipers, it may vibrate its tail and gape menacingly when threatened.

Night adders
Subfamily *Causinae*

Six species of night adder, all within the single genus *Causus*, are found only in Africa, south of the Sahara Desert. The most widespread species is the rhombic night adder (*C. rhombeatus*), which occurs throughout the larger part of the continent. They have smooth scales, symmetrically-arranged on the crown of the head, and eyes with round pupils, and thus differ from most other vipers

ABOVE: **Velvety night adder, *Causus resimus*.**

in overall appearance. Night adders are also among the few species of viper that lay eggs as opposed to bearing live, fully developed young. Typically less than 80 cm (30 in) long, most are brown or grey, with patterns of spots or blotches. The snout of an East African species, *C. defilippi*, is upturned and perhaps used for rooting out its prey. Although comparatively inoffensive, when thoroughly aroused night adders draw the body into a defensive coil, inflate themselves with air, and emit a surprisingly loud, guttural hiss.

Night adders have large venom glands. Their venom is especially toxic to toads, their natural prey, but appears to be rather less dangerous to humans than that of other vipers.

LEFT: **Rhombic night adder, *Causus rhombeatus*. Night adders are terrestrial snakes that feed largely on amphibians, especially toads.**

Which snake is the most dangerous?

In answer to the frequently asked question of which snake in the world has the most lethal venom, the outright winner is the inland taipan or fierce snake (*Oxyuranus microlepidotus*), an Australian relative of the cobras. The venom of this species is considerably more toxic than that of any other snake – a single bite delivers enough to kill more than 200,000 mice, or at least 12 adult men. Whether or not this species is the most dangerous in terms of the everyday lives of humans, however, is a different matter. Inland taipans are shy and rarely encountered snakes found only in the remote outback of western Queensland, where few people have ever even see one.

The group of species responsible for the greatest number of fatal accidents, and thus overall probably the most dangerous of all venomous snakes, are the saw-scaled or carpet vipers (*Echis*). These widely distributed snakes are found throughout much of northern Africa, the Middle East, India and Asia, often in close proximity to human habitation, and in places they may be remarkably abundant. Owing to their small size and highly cryptic colour pattern, they are difficult to detect and may easily be stepped on. They also have an exceptionally toxic venom, and their dangerous nature is further enhanced by the fact that they are short-tempered and will strike out with little provocation. Among various other formidably dangerous species responsible for a large proportion of snake-bite fatalities in humans are the Neotropical lanceheads (*Bothrops*) from Central and South America, the puff adder (*Bitis arietans*) and mambas (*Dendroaspis*) of Africa, the cobras (*Naja*) of Africa, India, and Southeast Asia, Russell's viper (*Daboia russelli*) of India and Southeast Asia, and in the New Guinea and Australian region, death adders (*Acanthophis*), the common taipan (*Oxyuranus scutellatus*), the tiger snake (*Notechis scutatus*), and brown snakes (*Pseudonaja*).

Bites from venomous snakes are in some parts of the world a major health risk, and on average are believed to cause the death of 50,000–100,000 people each year. They are clearly a significant threat to the safety and livelihoods of humans, especially those living in rural areas where snakes are more likely to be encountered and medical help in the event of an accident may be many hours or even days away. It would be wrong to assume, however, that the bite of a dangerously venomous snake has only one inevitable outcome. The percentage of deaths reported each year in relation to the actual number of people bitten is actually very small, and one need look at the details of only a few case histories to appreciate that the symptoms and severity of snakebite depend on a wide range of circumstances. These include the size of the snake in question (from a small juvenile to a large adult), quantity of venom injected, individual sensitivity of the victim, level of medical care and time taken to reach hospital, to name only a few. Even if one is unfortunate enough to be bitten by a venomous snake, this does not necessarily always lead to the injection of venom and the development of poisoning symptoms. Venom is a precious commodity that requires energy and time to produce and, as their principal means of obtaining food, most snakes will not expend it needlessly when defending themselves. Based on studies of proven bites by particular species, the ratio of bites to envenomation is usually about 2:1.

BELOW: **Asian saw-scaled viper, *Echis carinatus*.**

True vipers
Subfamily *Viperinae*

The true vipers, of which there are some 63 species divided among 13 genera, are restricted to the Old World regions of Europe, Asia, and Africa. They differ most conspicuously from New World vipers in lacking facial heat-sensitive pits.

RIGHT: **The adder,** *Vipera berus*, **is one of the world's most successful snakes. It has the largest geographical distribution of any terrestrial land-living species, ranging from the British Isles, across Europe and northern Asia, east to the Pacific Ocean, and also occurs further north than any other snake. Adders exhibit considerable colour dimorphism; above, reproductively active male; centre, female; bottom, year-old juvenile.**

Twenty-five species of the genus *Vipera* occur mostly in Europe and parts of Asia, where in places (such as Britain) they are the only dangerous snakes. They are all fairly heavy-bodied snakes with short tails, well defined, triangular heads, relatively large head scales, and a distinctive zigzag pattern along the body. Some species, such as the nose-horned viper (*V. ammodytes*) have a scaly 'nose-horn' on the tip of the snout. Terrestrial, they occur in a variety of habitats including open forests, sandy heaths, wet meadows, and dry rocky hillsides. Two particularly widespread species, the European viper or adder (*V. berus*) and asp viper (*V. aspis*) are found up to about 3000 m (10,000 ft) in the European Alps. All species are active by day, although at least some become partly nocturnal when night-time temperatures are high enough. Most hibernate during winter, often in communal dens, and after emerging in spring some migrate short distances to different feeding grounds. While most feed on rodents and lizards, the small meadow viper (*V. ursinii*) mainly eats insects. Four similar species in the genus *Macrovipera* are larger snakes characterized by small head scales.

Among the most dangerous of all snakes are the eight species of saw-scaled or carpet vipers (*Echis*) from North Africa, the Middle East, India and Asia, which are responsible for several thousand snakebite fatalities each year. When alarmed, these irascible little snakes rub the coils of their bodies together, producing a curious rasping sound.

The ten species of African bush vipers (*Atheris*) and the monotypic Uzungwe viper

RIGHT: **Great Lakes bush viper, *Atheris nitschei*, an East African species often found in the peripheral forests around Lake Victoria and other large lakes. The milky-coloured eyes are a symptom of the skin-shedding process.**

BELOW: **Although not a pit viper, the facial nerve endings in Russell's viper, *Daboia russelli*, are highly sensitive to temperature variation. Several other snakes that lack pits also have heat-sensitive areas on their heads, including puff adders (*Bitis arietans*) and *Boa constrictor*.**

(*Adenorhinos barbouri*) from Tanzania are distinctive-looking snakes with short, rounded heads and large eyes. Some are brightly coloured and have peculiarly fringed scales. Found in the equatorial forests of Africa, most are tree-dwellers. Two related species, Hindi's viper (*Montatheris hindii*) from high-altitude moorlands in Kenya, and the lowland swamp viper (*Proatheris superciliaris*) from Mozambique, Malawi, and Tanzania, are terrestrial.

Fourteen species in the exclusively African genus *Bitis* are exceptionally stout-bodied vipers with broad, flattened, triangular heads. All are strictly terrestrial. With a distribution extending throughout Africa and into southern Arabia, the puff adder (*B. arietans*) is the most common and widespread, while the massively built Gaboon viper (*B. gabonica*) is the largest, attaining lengths of almost 2 m (6.6 ft) and weights of over 10 kg (22 lb)! This formidable snake has been known to eat small antelopes and even porcupines. Gaboon vipers and a similar-looking species, the river jack (*B. nasicornis*), are tropical-forest-dwellers with curious scaly horns on the tip of the snout and camouflaging colour patterns that resemble dead leaves. Other species, such as Peringuey's adder (*B. peringueyi*), are small desert-dwellers with conspicuous horn-like projections over the eyes, a feature they share with five species of African and Asian sand vipers (*Cerastes* and *Pseudocerastes*). Macmahon's viper (*Eristicophis macmahoni*), a similarly unusual species from western Pakistan, has peculiar, whorl-like rows of heavily keeled scales, with a shovel-shaped rostral scale. Many of these desert-dwelling vipers have developed a unique sidewinding method of progression to overcome the difficulties of moving across loose, shifting sand (see p. 14).

BELOW: **Horned sand viper, *Cerastes cerastes*. This desert species buries itself in sand where it lies in wait for prey with only its eyes and nostrils visible.**

Rattlesnakes and other pit vipers
Subfamily *Crotalinae*

Species in this subfamily include the rattlesnakes and about 15 other genera distributed throughout the Americas and southern Asia. Their most characteristic feature is a pair of heat-sensitive pit organs on each side of the head used for locating prey (which most pythons and some boas of the genera *Corallus*, *Epicrates*, and *Boa* also have). In pythons and boas they occur on or between the scales of the lips (labials), while the vipers have a single pit on each side of the face between the eye and nostril. Those of the pit vipers are more sophisticated in that they consist of two compartments, divided in the middle by a membranous diaphragm. The smaller, inner part is connected by a narrow duct to a small pore in front of the eye, which appears to be a means of balancing the air pressure on either side of the diaphragm, and also records the ambient air temperature. The larger outer chamber opens as a wide, forwardly directed aperture, through which infrared radiation emitted by prey enters

and is detected by a series of highly sensitive thermoreceptive cells.

The heat-sensitive pits of snakes are extraordinarily sensitive to temperature variation, and experiments have shown that those of some pit vipers can detect changes in temperature of as little as 0.001°C (0.002°F). Using these organs, the snake can locate prey, or enemies, even in complete darkness. A pit viper deprived of its senses of sight and smell, for example, can perceive a mouse 10°C (18°F) warmer than its surroundings from a distance of 70 cm (28 in), and guide the direction of its strike accordingly to within about 5°.

Rattlesnakes, of which there are 32 species, mostly in the genus *Crotalus*, are inhabitants of dry woodlands, prairies and rocky desert environments, mainly in North America and Mexico. One species, the cascabel (*C. durissus*), ranges through southern Central America into South America, while the Uracoan rattlesnake (*C. vegrandis*) from eastern Venezuela is restricted to that country. They are all rather stout-bodied snakes that range in length from the three 60 cm (2 ft) long pygmy rattlesnakes (*Sistrurus*) to the big eastern

FAR LEFT: **Timber rattlesnake, *Crotalus horridus*. During the winter months large numbers of this eastern north American species hibernate underground in rocky dens, often communally with rat snakes, copperheads, and other snakes.**

LEFT: **The heat-sensory pit in this cascabel or Neotropical rattlesnake, *Crotalus durissus*, can be seen clearly as a dark hole in the side of the face.**

The vipers of Queimada Grande

A small, deserted island off the eastern coast of Brazil barely 1 km (0.6 mile) across at its widest point, Queimada Grande is a refuge for large numbers of birds. It is renowned mostly, however, for its other main inhabitant, an endemic species of pit viper which occurs in extraordinary abundance. The golden lancehead (*Bothrops insularis*) is a slender and unusually pale-coloured species that probably diverged from its larger mainland relative, the jararaca (*Bothrops jararaca*), when the island broke away from the Brazilian coast about 11,000 years ago. It subsists almost entirely on the various species of small birds that use the island as a reviving 'stop-off' point while on migration, and relies on its potent, fast-acting venom to kill prey before they have a chance to fly away.

Walking through the island's wooded interior, it is not unusual to spot a golden lancehead every few paces. Commonly seen in trees, they may also be encountered among leaves on the ground, nestled between tree roots, on rock faces, and in almost every other accessible habitat. That so many of these snakes should occur in an area so small seems remarkable. There are, however, no other kinds of venomous snakes on Queimada Grande with which the lancehead might otherwise need to compete for food and shelter, and neither does it have any significant predators. With a more or less regular supply of birds, its principal food source is also almost always available.

Golden lanceheads are undoubtedly dangerous snakes, but contrary to popular belief, their venom is in fact less lethal than that of many mainland *Bothrops* species, including its presumed nearest relative, *B. jararaca*, at least as assessed by mouse LD_{50} tests. The erroneous reputation of high lethality in the venom of this species appears to have originated from some late 19th century experiments without details of methods. There have been several repeated experiments in recent years in which the reported high lethality of *B. insularis* venom has not been replicated. It would be interesting to know whether the venom of this species is relatively more lethal to birds, its natural prey.

LEFT: **Golden lancehead,** *Bothrops insularis*.

diamondback (*Crotalus adamanteus*), which may exceed 2 m (6.6 ft). In newborn snakes the characteristic tail rattle, from which theses pit vipers take their name, is at first only a small button. Additional segments accumulate with successive moults of the skin, and when the rattle becomes too large, the last and oldest segments break off. The rattle is used only for defence and at least one species, the Santa Catalina Island rattlesnake (*C. catalinensis*), has lost it, the probable reason being that having no natural predators, this species has little need for such an adaptation.

None of the remaining pit viper genera have rattles, although many will vibrate their tails among dry leaves when alarmed, which has the effect of creating a similar sound. Among the most diverse of the Latin American forms are 41 species of fer-de-lance (*Bothrops*) named after their characteristic lance-shaped heads. All are highly dangerous and they include such notorious species as the terciopelo (*B. asper*) from Mexico and Central America, and the South American jararaca (*B. jararaca*) and urutu (*B. alternatus*). So feared is the bite of the bushmaster (*Lachesis*), the world's largest viper that in parts of its range it has been given the name matabuey, meaning 'ox-killer'. Bushmasters have rather peculiar knob-like scales and they share this feature with jumping vipers (*Atropoides*), a group of three exceptionally stout-bodied snakes named for their ability to strike with such force that the body is often carried forward with the momentum. Other ground-dwelling pit vipers from the Americas include three species of the genus *Agkistrodon*, of which the copperhead (*A. contortrix*) is an abundant species found over much of the eastern United States, and the cottonmouth (*A. piscivorous*) is unique among vipers in being semi-aquatic. Eight hognosed pit vipers (*Porthidium*) are inhabitants mostly of lowland tropical forests, while two species of Mexican horned vipers (*Ophryacus*) and three of montane pit vipers (*Cerrophidion*) live high in the mountains of southern Mexico and Central America. Nine species of palm vipers (*Bothriechis*) are climbers, characterized by slender bodies, strongly prehensile tails, and beautifully mottled green color patterns that are perhaps unsurpassed in concealing these snakes among leafy trees.

Old World pit vipers include the ecologically diverse genus *Trimeresurus*, with 28 species distributed throughout much of Asia, India, and numerous islands in the western Pacific Ocean. Most of these are tree-climbers and many, such as Pope's pit viper (*T. popeiorum*) and the Chinese pit

RIGHT: **Greatest of the pit vipers and largest of all venomous snakes in the Western Hemisphere, the bushmaster may reach an adult size of more than 3.5 m (11.5 ft). Three species are recognized, of which this example, from Ecuador, is the common form,** *Lachesis muta*.

LEFT: **Malayan pit viper,** *Calloselasma rhodostoma.* **This dangerously venomous species is found throughout much of Southeast Asia, but despite its common name it occurs in only a small part of peninsular Malaysia.**

viper (*T. albolabris*), have characteristic leaf-green colour patterns. Among the largest is the habu (*T. flavoviridis*), which may attain lengths of 2.2 m (7 ft). Two similar Southeast Asian species separated in the genus *Tropidolaemus* are distinguished from other forms by keeled chin scales, and include the strikingly marked temple viper (*T. wagleri*).

Of various ground-dwelling pit vipers known from Asia, five exceptionally thick-bodied species of *Ovophis* include the Ryukyu Island pit viper (*O. okinavensis*) restricted to this island in the Japanese Pacific, and mountain pit viper (*O. monticola*), a species found throughout much of Asia, from India to China and Taiwan. Three species of hump-nosed vipers (*Hypnale*) from southwestern

India and Sri Lanka and the hundred-pace viper (*Deinagkistrodon acutus*) from southeastern China and Taiwan are tropical forest forms characterized by upturned snouts, and ten species of *Gloydius* are small inhabitants of temperate forests and mountains in western and southern Asia. One of these, *G. himalayanus*, occurs up to 4900 m (16,000 ft) in the Himalayas. Among the most dangerous of the Asian pit vipers is the Malayan pit viper (*Calloselasma rhodostoma*), a tropical forest species which is widespread in Southeast Asia and the cause of many snakebite accidents in this region. In common with a number of other Asian pit vipers, and unlike most of its New World relatives, it is an egg-layer.

Glossary

adaptive radiation: the development of related species over time into differently-adapted forms

aestivation: an extended period of dormancy during periods of heat or drought

aglyphous: applied to snakes that have regular dentition; i.e. lacking modified venom-conducting teeth (see p. 8)

aposematic colouration: colour and patterning designed to advertise the toxic or dangerous nature of an animal

aquatic: living in fresh water

arboreal: tree-living

autohaemorrage: spontaneous bleeding behaviour that has evolved in some snakes (e.g. genus *Tropidophis*) probably as a means of evading predators

autotomy: the ability to shed a part of the body, usually the tail, either spontaneously or when grasped by a predator

chemoreception: odour detection; pertaining to the senses of taste and smell

cloaca: the common chamber into which the reproductive and digestive tracts discharge their contents, emptying outside through the vent

constriction: method of killing prey whereby the victim is held very tightly within the snake's coils so that breathing is prevented

convergent evolution: term applied to unrelated species that have acquired similar appearances and behaviours in response to a similar way of life

coronoid: a small bone of the lower jaw found in some primitive snakes (see p. 9)

dentary: the front, tooth-bearing part of a snake's lower jaw bone (see p. 9)

diurnal: active during the day

Duvernoy's gland: venom-producing gland of rear-fanged colubrid snakes, named after D.M. Duvernoy, a French anatomist

ectopterygoid: a bone in the upper jaw forming part of the biting mechanism (see p. 9)

haemotoxic: term used to describe the action

of a poison that primarily attacks the blood and circulatory system

hemipenis (*pl.* hemipenes): one of the paired male reproductive organs of snakes (see p. 7)

herpetology: the study of amphibians and reptiles

hibernation: an extended period of dormancy during the winter

hypapophysis: the ventral projection on a vertebrae

internasals: a typically paired set of scales on the top of a snake's snout between its nostrils

labials: scales lining the edge of a snake's upper and lower jaw

loreal scale: a scale on the side of a snake's snout between the nostril and eye, but usually touching neither

marine: living in sea water

maxilla: the bone in the forward part of a snake's upper jaw to which the venom-conducting fangs (where present) are attached (see p. 8, 9)

melanophores: pigment-containing organelles in the skin

mental groove: a lengthwise cleft between the scales on the underside of a snake's chin

mimicry: a species that resembles another, often distasteful or harmful species

monotypic: term used to describe a genus represented by only a single species

myotoxic: term used to describe a poison that destroys muscle tissue

neural spine: the dorsal projection on a vertebrae

neurotoxic: term used to describe a poison that has a particularly marked (although often not exclusive) effect on the nerve tissues

Old World: the continents of the Eastern hemisphere known before the discovery of the Americas, i.e. Europe, Asia, and Africa

opisthoglyphous: term applied to snakes having fangs toward the back of the mouth; syn. rear-fanged (see p. 8)

oviparous: egg-laying

palaeophid: of the family Palaeophiidae, an extinct group of snakes that lived during the Lower Eocene period and are related to modern-day boas

palatine: a bone of the inner palate that in many snakes bears teeth (see p. 9)

parthenogenesis: reproduction without males; females produce genetically identical young from unfertilized eggs

postfrontal: a bone in the upper part of the head found in some primitive snakes (see p. 9)

premaxilla: a small bone on the end of the snout that in some primitive snakes bears small teeth (see p. 9)

procrypsis: colour and patterning designed to conceal an animal in its natural habitat

proteroglyphous: term applied to snakes having fangs in the front of the mouth that are largely immovable (see p. 8)

pterygoid: a tooth-bearing bone in the back of the upper jaw (see p. 9)

rear-fanged: a non-zoological but useful term applied to any snake with enlarged venom-conducting teeth in the rear of the upper jaw (*syn.* opisthoglyphous)

rostral scale: the scale at the tip of a snake's snout

solenoglyphous: term applied to snakes having fangs in the front of the mouth that are hinged and erectile (see p. 8)

stapes: a small bony rod at the back of the skull through which sound vibrations are transmitted to the inner ear (see p. 9)

supratemporal: a bone that links the quadrate and lower jaw assembly in snakes with the back of the skull (see p. 9)

tracheal lung: an additional respiratory organ of snakes attached to the windpipe

viviparous: live-bearing; applied to species in which the female retains the eggs internally and gives birth when the young are fully developed

Index

Note: Index includes common names of snakes, and main references for general subject matter (see under specific snakes for further information). Where there is more than one reference under a specific snake, bold indicates main reference. Italics indicate feature boxes.

Further Information

Further Reading

Australian snakes: a natural history, Richard Shine. Reed Books, Sydney, 1991.

The dangerous snakes of Africa, Stephen Spawls and Bill Branch. Blandford Press, London, 1995.

The encyclopaedia of snakes, Chris Mattison. Blandford Press, London, 1995.

Rattlesnake: portrait of a predator, Manny Rubio. Smithsonian Institution Press, Washington, 1998.

Sea snakes, 2nd edn., Harold Heatwole. Krieger and University of New South Wales, 1999.

Snakes: the evolution of mystery in nature, Harry Greene. University of California Press, Berkeley, 1997.

Snakes: a natural history, H.W. Parker and A.G.C. Grandison. Cornell University Press and The Natural History Museum, London, 1977.

Snakes in question: the Smithsonian answer book, Carl H. Ernst and George R. Zug. Smithsonian Institution Press, Washington, 1996.

Tales of giant snakes: a historical natural history of anacondas and pythons, John C. Murphy and Robert W. Henderson. Krieger, 1997.

The venomous reptiles of Latin America, Jonathan A. Campbell and William W. Lamar. Ithaca, New York, 1989.

Herpetological Societies

Australasian Affiliation of Herpetological Societies
P.O. Box R307, Royal Exchange, Sydney 2000, Australia.

British Herpetological Society
c/o Zoological Society of London, Regent's Park, London, NW1 4RY, UK
http://www.thebhs.org

European Snake Society
Van Nesstraat 13A, 3814 RS Amersfoort, The Netherlands.
http://home.wxs.nl/~onbek109/

Herpetological Association of Africa
P.O. Box 20142, Durban North 4016, South Africa.

German Society for Herpetology
(Deutsche Gesellschaft für Herpetologie und Terrarienkunde)
Wormersdorfer Str. 46–48, D–53359 Rheinbach, Germany
http://www.dght.de/english.htm

Society for the Study of Amphibians and Reptiles
c/o Saint Louis University, Dept. of Biology, 3507 Laclede, St. Louis, MO 63103–2010 USA. http://www.ukans.edu/~ssar/.

Internet Resources

EMBL reptile database
http://www.embl-heidelberg.de/~uetz/LivingReptiles.html
[a comprehensive listing of all reptile species with full details of distribution and classification]

WWW Virtual Library; herpetology
http://cmgm.stanford.edu/~meisen/herp/
[links to sites on the herpetological sites on the web]

Links to various herpetological societies and organizations web sites
http://www.onrampinc.net/mhs/herpsoc.htm
http://www.tinygiants.com/links/Herp_Societies/
http://www.corallus.com/societies.html

Combined index to herpetological collections
http://research.calacademy.org/herpetology/Comb_Herp_Index.html
[a searchable list of scientific snake collections in the USA]

Snakebite protocol
http://www-surgery.ucsd.edu/ent/davidson/Snake/index.htm
[detailed treatment procedures for bites from venomous snakes]

Snakes in captivity
http://www.kingsnake.com/

[features links to discussion lists focussing on the captive maintenance and biology of particular species groups]
http://www.halcyon.com/slavens/breeding.html
[provides information on breeding and longevity of amphibians and reptiles in captivity]

Snakes in general: http://www.thesnake.org/
African bush vipers: http://hometown.aol.com/squamigers/page/index.htm
Australian snakes: http://www.nettrek.com.au/~bush/index.html
http://www.kingsnake.com/australia/index.htm
Cottonmouths: http://gto.ncsa.uiuc.edu/pingleto/herps/Fieldnotes/shawnee/intro.html
King cobra: http://www.nationalgeographic.com/features/97/kingcobra/index-ie.html
Mambas: http://www.kingsnake.com/mamba/
Rattlesnakes: http://www.rattlesnakes.com/
South American pit vipers: http://eco.ib.usp.br/labvert/Jararaca-Ingles/ingles-proj-jar-principal.htm
Tree boas: http://www.frontiernet.net/~rsajdak/grenada/grenada.htm

NB Web addresses are subject to change.

Picture credits

Unless otherwise stated, illustrations are copyright of The Natural History Museum, London.

pp 48, 60, 61, 62 Bill Branch
p 56 Jonathan Campbell / University of Texas at Arlington
p 20 John Cann
pp 14, 15, 30, 37, 43 (top), 53, 55, 68, 71 (top, bottom), 75, 87 (bottom), 105 Chris Mattison
pp 40, 50 (top), 70, 92, 93 Mark O'Shea
pp 24, 79, 99 (top) Stephen Spawls
pp 5, 12, 16, 18, 22, 23 (top, bottom), 26, 36, 38 (top, bottom), 39 (top, bottom), 41, 42 (top, bottom), 44, 49, 50 (bottom), 63, 64, 65, 66 (top), 67 (top), 69, 73 (bottom), 76 (top), 77, 82 (+ inset), 83, 84, 85, 97 (top), 101 (top, middle, bottom) Peter Stafford, The Natural History Museum
pp 29 (bottom), 47, 91, 94, 96 Stephen Swanson
pp 25, 27, 28 (top), 32 (bottom), 34, 35, 43 (bottom), 45 (top, bottom), 46, 54, 57, 66 (bottom), 72, 76 (bottom), 80, 88, 89, 90 (top, bottom), 98 (bottom), 99 (bottom), 102 (top), 103, 108 Stephen Von Peltz
pp 11 (bottom), 17, 19, 32 (top), 67 (bottom), 73 (top), 78, 81 (top left and right), 86, 87 (top), 98 (top), 100, 102 (bottom), 104 (left, right), 106, 107 Wolfgang Wüster

Author's acknowledgements

For help in reviewing parts of this book during its preparation the author is indebted to Colin McCarthy and Garth Underwood (Department of Zoology, The Natural History Museum, London), Robert Henderson (Milwaukee Public Museum, USA), and Wolfgang Wüster (School of Biological Sciences, University of Wales). Grateful thanks are also due to David Bird (Poole Serpentarium, Dorset), David Feldmar, David House, Anthony Graham, and the Zoological Society of London, who assisted in a variety of different ways, and to Stephen Von Peltz, without whose generous support in helping to offset production costs the book could not have progressed so easily to fruition.